# Ti Liv Kréyòl

## A LEARNER'S GUIDE TO LOUISIANA CREOLE

ADRIEN GUILLORY-CHATMAN
OLIVER MAYEUX
NATHAN WENDTE
HERBERT WILTZ

ILLUSTRATIONS BY
JONATHAN "RADBWA FAROUSH" MAYERS

DESIGN BY
IRINA V. WANG

Guillory-Chatman, Adrien, Oliver Mayeux, Nathan Wendte, and Herbert J. Wiltz. 2020. *Ti Liv Kréyòl: A Learner's Guide to Louisiana Creole.* Second edition. New Orleans: TSÒHK.

# Introduction 4–12

# Lessons 13–88



# Grammar Sketch 89–122



# Lexicon 123–165



# More Resources 166–168

# Introduction

## *About This Book & Who We Are*

# *ALON KOMENSÉ.* LET'S BEGIN.

*Éy laba!* Hey there! *Byinvini* and welcome to the second edition of the *Ti Liv Kréyòl*—'The Little Creole Book'—the first book for learning Louisiana Creole, an endangered language born in Louisiana that is also known as Kouri-Vini.

The first edition of the *Ti Liv Kréyòl* was released as a public domain e-book in 2017. You may be reading this second edition on the computer, or holding it in your hands — we have made it available for free online and for a low cost in print. All profits from the sales of this book will go towards distributing print copies of the book in historically Creole-speaking communities and towards supporting future activities to revitalize the language. In this edition, we've worked hard to ensure consistency with other available language resources. We've also added a new Grammar Sketch, improved the lexicon, and created audio recordings of each dialogue which are available for free online at www.learnlouisianacreole.com

### *ÇA TO VA TROUVÉ DAN LIV-ÇILA.* WHAT YOU WILL FIND IN THIS BOOK.

- 18 lessons, with dialogues and glossaries covering a range of topics
- An all-new Grammar Sketch, providing a basic overview of how the language works
- Creole-English glossary and English-Creole glossaries, containing thousands of words: all of the words in the lessons, many more useful terms and a few fun favorites thrown in as *lañap* (lagniappe — an added extra)
- Audio recordings of all the dialogues available for free online at www.learnlouisianacreole.com

## *KOMEN IZÉ LIV-ÇILA*. HOW TO USE THIS BOOK.

Whenever trying to use an unfamiliar language to communicate, a degree of accommodation is required. The variety of language taught in this *Ti Liv Kréyòl* will — with a little effort — allow you to communicate effectively with any other speaker of Louisiana Creole.

**WHAT THIS BOOK WILL DO:**

- Give learners the tools to communicate with other speakers of Louisiana Creole
- Provide SOME information on the variation present within the language

**WHAT THIS BOOK WILL *NOT* DO:**

- Cover ALL variants of the language
- Please everybody

Louisiana Creole (a.k.a. Kouri-Vini) is an endangered language formerly spoken to varying degrees in Louisiana and the greater Gulf South. Today, the language survives in isolated pockets of Louisiana and in diaspora communities in Texas, California, Illinois, and elsewhere. Because of the fragmented nature of the speech community, as well as internal variation within the language itself, a great amount of diversity exists at every level. This diversity also reflects the fact that many Louisiana Creole speakers were historically multilingual or multi-lectal (able to speak/understand more than one dialect). Differences between individual communities were the norm, not the exception. The language variety presented here is only one of many historically spoken by Gulf South Creoles.

The alphabet used throughout this book is based on a variant proposed by Landry et al. (2016). Since their alphabet was meant to be mostly phonetic, some words presented in this work will have alternate pronunciations/forms depending on the speaker. For teaching purposes, we have generally tried to use only one written form for every word. Most variants will pose no difficulty to a learner as they vary only slightly. This is not a textbook in the strictest since; rather, it is intended to furnish the words and the structures necessary to create natural sentences in Louisiana Creole. It is a primer, not an exhaustive guide to the language.

# *KI NO YÊ*. WHO WE ARE.

The *Ti Liv Kréyòl* was put together by a team of people over a couple of years. It was the brainchild of linguist **NATHAN WENDTE** who produced a first draft of the lessons and lexicon in early 2017. Linguist **OLIVER MAYEUX** then joined to help edit these. Nathan and Oliver worked together with long-time champion of Creole language and culture, **HERBERT JOSEPH WILTZ**, who reviewed the manuscript of the first edition and made invaluable edits based on his experience as a native speaker of the language and a high school teacher. At that time, the manuscript was also sent around to different community organizations and individuals so that different opinions on the work could be gathered. The first edition of the *Ti Liv Kréyòl* saw the light of day in August 2017!

In 2018, The Foundation for Endangered Languages awarded a small grant for the production of a new and improved print edition of the book. It was at this point that **ADRIEN GUILLORY-CHATMAN** joined the team. As both a long-time learner of the language and as an educator, Adrien made sure the book was presented in a consistent way that would be accessible and helpful for as many people as possible. Graphic designer and language enthusiast **IRINA V. WANG** also came onboard, bringing her expertise on designing learning materials for endangered languages. Irina put together the finished product you are now reading, which we hope you will agree is beautifully presented. Of course, a huge part of the look and feel of this second edition comes from the original illustrations by Louisiana Creole artist, writer, curator and language activist **JONATHAN "RADBWA FAROUSH" MAYERS**. Additionally, Herbert Wiltz and Nathan recorded the audio resources and edited the dialogues. Oliver and Nathan co-authored the all-new grammar sketch. Oliver edited the lexicon and, together with Nathan and Adrien, checked for consistency. At all stages of the project, we received invaluable feedback from a number of people including Christophe Landry, members of C.R.E.O.L.E., Inc., and members of Latab Kréyòl in Parks.

If you have your own feedback or just want to say *bonjou*, we would love to hear from you. Go ahead and write us at lacreoleprimer@gmail.com

## ADRIEN GUILLORY-CHATMAN

Adrien Guillory-Chatman is an educator and former school administrator who is a native of Lafayette, Louisiana and lives in the Chicago area. While growing up in Chicago, Kouri-Vini and Louisiana French languages were spoken by her family as well as some neighbors and fellow parishioners. Although Adrien understood the adults around her, she herself only spoke some phrases and words as a child. She always longed to fluently speak the languages of her ancestors. In 2013, she had the opportunity to begin the lifelong journey of learning/relearning Kouri-Vini. Today, her passion lies in assisting others to reclaim their heritage languages, especially individuals who reside in the Louisiana Diaspora. Adrien helps to organize Kouri-Vini tables in Chicago. She is a contributor to various Kouri-Vini forums on social media and created a series of Kouri-Vini family card games. Currently, Adrien is designing a website where children can learn Louisiana Creole.

## HERBERT WILTZ

Born in Breaux Bridge, Louisiana in St. Martin Parish, Herbert was reared by his grandparents. It was there that he heard, on a daily basis, the Creole language spoken by all who came to his grandparents' home. His parents resided in Houston, Texas. Throughout his childhood, he communicated with family members, neighbors and peers using the Creole language. He later earned a four year scholarship to attend Southern University where he majored in French with a minor in Spanish. During his tenure at Southern, he traveled to France and studied at L'Universite Catholique d'Angers in Angers, France. This was a CODOFIL French Study Program. Herbert earned a Masters Degree in French and Spanish and a Masters Degree in Administration and Supervision. He would return to his high school, Holy Rosary Institute, to teach French and Spanish and served as an Assistant Principal. He was an assistant Principal at Lafayette High School from 1996-1998 and appointed Principal at Immaculate Heart of Mary School from 2003-2005. He also studied and toured Guadeloupe and Martinique on a scholarship sponsored by CODOFIL.

Herbert's knowledge of French and Spanish afforded him the opportunity to demonstrate the many ways to use the languages outside of the educational arena. He served as Master of Ceremony for many festivals, such as Festival International and Louisiana Zydeco Music Festival. He served on the Board of Directors of Festival International de Louisiane. He hosted a KRVS Zydeco radio show called "Les Haricots Sont Pas Salés" for thirteen years. He was cast as "JoJo" in a French speaking play "Les Attakapas" presented by Mr. James Fontenot. He has participated on various panel discussions. For three years he presented information on the Creole Culture sponsored by the New Orleans Jazz Fest. He was invited to participate on a panel at the Smithsonian Institute in Washington, D.C. on the "Modern Migrations and Identity in the African Diaspora." He authored and was the featured narrator of Episode 10 of the French speaking video series "Gumb-oh! Là! Là!" This was a personal narrative on Louisiana Creoles presented by Charles Laroque. He assisted Mr. Roy Williams with French terminology of his children's book, "Bouki's Honey: The Creole Folktales of Bouki & Lapin." He has assisted in various presentations at Creole Day sponsored by Vermilionville.

In 1988, Herbert met and married his high school sweetheart, Sueline Taylor. He also joined the Lafayette Parish School System where he taught Spanish for twelve years. During this time he assisted in the creation of C.R.E.O.L.E., Inc. (Cultural, Resourceful, Educational Opportunities toward Linguistic Enrichment, Incorporated). He served as President and continues to be an active member. He was named Teacher of the Year in 1992 for Comeaux High School and in 2007 for Milton Elementary/Middle School. In that Creole was only considered an oral language, an important project to Herbert was the creation of Creole lessons written over a span of three years. These were published in the monthly Creole Magazine created by Ruth Foote. To date, these lessons, with modifications, are being used to educate individuals interested in learning Louisiana Creole and also served as inspiration for parts of this book.

Herbert is the recipient of many awards. In 2006, he was awarded the Richard Catalon award at Vermilionville during the annual Creole Day celebration. He was also awarded the Citizen Award presented by councilmen Chris Williams and Louis Benjamin. He retired from the Lafayette Parish School

System in May, 2015. His future endeavor is to envision the creation of a Creole curriculum that will be used by various learning institutions as a vehicle to preserve the Louisiana Creole language. Herbert writes: "The language I heard and spoke at home, in the streets, in the stores and even at school during recess was Kréyòl. Native of Breaux Bridge, LA in the parish of St. Martin, I, Herbert Joseph Wiltz, was drawn to this language at an early age. Everyone who visited my grandparents' home communicated using Kréyòl. I was immersed in the language in that I heard it everyday. As well noted, Kréyòl was considered an oral language. It was in the 1990's that I decided to put into words what I heard spoken in the regions where I grew up. Up to that time very little written resources existed. I wanted to showcase what the spoken Louisiana Kréyòl language may have looked like. I began to write vocabulary listings, dialogs and lessons that were published in the monthly Creole Magazine created by Ruth Foote. I felt that it was important to preserve the language as it was considered a dying language. Many of the younger generation did not speak Kréyòl with their parents. Presently I have collaborated with Nathan Wendte, Oliver Mayeux and Adrien Guillory-Chatman in the creation of the *Ti Liv Kréyòl* which is a guide to teach, learn, and speak Kréyòl."

## OLIVER MAYEUX

On one side, Oliver's family are from Louisiana, on the other they are British; he grew up in Scotland and Nigeria. He has been interested in the Louisiana Creole language since his teenage years. He wrote his PhD thesis on the history and development of the language.

## NATHAN WENDTE

An avid language learner hailing from the Chicago suburbs, Nathan grew interested in Louisiana Creole after spending a year in Haiti and moving to New Orleans. His PhD dissertation compares and contrasts the Creole communities of Southeast Texas and Southwest Louisiana. He currently resides *Envil* with his wife and son.

## ILLUSTRATOR: JONATHAN MAYERS

Louisiana Creole artist, writer, and independent curator, Jonathan Mayers, was born and raised in Istrouma (Baton Rouge), Louisiana. His cultural heritage includes speakers of Louisiana Creole that lived and worked in Pointe Coupée and the River Parishes. As an artist who grew up in a society that struggles to maintain its uniqueness due to industrialization, consumerism, capitalism, and racism, Mayers' priority is to create work which aims to reverse that Americanization and to prompt a dialogue on ethnic identity, interrelatedness, and unique cultural experiences. He paints vibrant landscapes ambiguous enough to evoke feelings of familiarity, wonder, and adventure, then makes the connection between reality and illusion by adorning his work with materials from those distinct locations linked to cultural heritage and historic social or environmental events. Mayers attempts to champion narrative fantasy and representational landscape painting, addressing human-inflicted and natural consequences through personification in mythological beasts, not unlike the physical manifestation of Godzilla as a metaphor for the consequences of nuclear testing and war, and spark heritage language (re) acquisition in Louisiana by writing trilingual micro stories.

Mayers earned his MFA degree from the University of New Orleans and his BFA degree in Painting and Drawing from LSU. He received scholarships to attend French Immersion at Université Sainte-Anne in Church Point, Nova Scotia, Canada from both Université Sainte-Anne (2015) and CODOFIL (2016). Mayers has exhibited works in multiple *Prospect New Orleans Satellites*, *Surreal Salons* and *Louisiana Contemporary*s, *Notes from the Artistic Underground*, *ART I-10*, *Tiercé*, and *Tallahassee International*. In Fall 2018 he was an artist-in-residence at A Studio in the Woods for *Adaptations: Living with Change*. Mayers has been influenced by internationally recognized writers, novelist Fabienne Kanor and poet Aurora Levins Morales, with whom he's bonded over shared cultural similarities. Aside from *Ti Liv Kréyòl*, His latest heritage language collaborative art projects include *Crébisse-monstre*, an all-natural sculptural performance work with multidisciplinary artist Géraldine Laurendeau, and *Kit pa ça filé Bayou!*, an art exhibition he was ask to create and record Louisiana Creole translations for, with Filipino-American artist John Yoyogi

Fortes. He had the honor to represent Louisiana on the international literary stage for La Dictée Francophone 2019 after Louisiana's adhesion to the Organisation internationale de la Francophonie by writing an open verse poem called *La Latanière*, which can be found in the online journal *Le Bourdon de la Louisiane*. Currently, Mayers is represented by Arthur Roger Gallery in New Orleans and is the curator of *Mythologies Louisianaises*, an artistic collaborative project which features a trilingual publication in French, Kouri-Vini (thanks to Louisiana Creole language activist, Clif St. Laurent), and English. His works are held in national and international collections including the Crescent Center in New Orleans and that of M. Le Consul Général de France, Vincent Sciama. He is also a member of the Luminous Lookout artist collective and writes music in Louisiana Creole with his cousin, Joseph B. Darensbourg, and father, Hans "Fritz" Mayers. You can learn more about his work at www.jonathanmayers.com

**DESIGNER: IRINA V. WANG**

Irina grew up Taiwanese-Floridian before moving to the UK for undergraduate studies and working as a graphic designer at Pentagram London. Combining a love of typography, language, and environmental philosophy, she has designed alongside native communities and linguists to revitalize endangered languages such as Marma (Chittagong Hill Tracts), Unangam Tunuu (Aleutian Islands), and A'ingae (Sucumbíos Province). Recognizing that language justice, environmental justice, and social justice are one demand arising from shared systemic issues, she pursued a masters in Industrial Design at Rhode Island School of Design (RISD) to develop transdisciplinary approaches for ethical and urgent systems-shifting. Object interventions—whether digital publications or physical tools—create leverage points for positive disruption within broader social, political, and economic contexts. In addition to indigenous language revitalization, she works on and writes about nuclear non-proliferation, just energy transitions, and agricultural carbon sequestration as a free agent shepherding change between public and private spheres. You can see more of her work online at irinavw.xyz

# Lesson 01

## *Alphabet, Pronunciation & Numbers*

ènn fèt

The alphabet used in this primer was laid out in 2016 by Dr. Christophe Landry and other members of the revitalization community.* This orthography borrows from the French and English alphabets as well as the alphabets used to represent other French-based creoles of the world. The form of the word gives certain clues to its etymology and helps give Louisiana Creole a distinctive look.

As we will state several times throughout this book, it is difficult to capture the richness of the Creole language on the page. Just how everyone cooks their gumbo in slightly different ways, across the Gulf South people pronounce Creole differently too. To take this dynamic, spoken language and turn it into the static, written word is a huge challenge. Should we come up with a 'middle ground' to use for writing, effectively making a 'standardized' Creole for reading and writing? If so, how do we choose just one pronunciation or grammatical form? Doesn't one single standard risk erasing all the diversity that makes Creole such an interesting and beautiful language? Nobody likes a bland gumbo! Instead, we suggest including all of Creole's distinctive flavors. This means that people spell words how *they* say them, obeying the rules of one simple system which we describe here. Think of it as a list of ingredients.

In this guide, we have tried our best to keep spellings consistent to help you at the beginning of your language-learning journey. Over time, as you learn more, you can experiment with spicing up your Creole from your family or friends. As everyone knows, gumbo tastes better with plenty of spice!

For example, in the vowels below, you'll notice that some of the sounds of Louisiana Creole don't have an equivalent in English. These are known as *rounded vowels*, and they were inherited from the French language. Not all speakers use these sounds, however. You may hear some speakers pronounce the word 'butter' as *dibœr*, while others might pronounce it *dibè*. No matter how you choose to learn it, you should still be well understood by most other Creole speakers.

* Landry, Christophe, Cliford St. Laurent, and Michael Gisclair. *Kouri-Vini: A Guide to Louisiana Creole Orthography*. Louisiana and Historic Cultural Vistas, 2016. www.mylhcv.com

# VOYÈL-YÉ (13)

| LETTER | EXAMPLE | DESCRIPTION | IPA |
|---|---|---|---|
| **A** | lak / *lake* | as in English *father* | [a, ɑ] |
| **Æ** | fræer / *brother* | as in English *apple* | [æ] |
| **E** | de / *two* | as in French *deux*; close to English *uh* | [ø] |
| **É** | lété / *summer* | as in English *pay*, but no <y> sound | [e] |
| **È** | fèt / *party* | as in English *let* | [ɛ] |
| **I** | gri / *gray* | as in English *fee* | [i] |
| **Ì** | babìnn / *lip* | as in English *it* | [ɪ] |
| **O** | gro / *large* | as in English *toe* | [o] |
| **Ò** | lòt / *another* | as in English *bought* | [ɔ] |
| **Œ** | sœr / *sister* | as in French *sœur*; no English equivalent | [œ] |
| **OU** | toujou / *always* | as in English *fool* | [u] |
| **U** | sûr / *sure* | as in French *sûr*; no English equivalent | [y] |

# KONSONN-YÉ (23)

| | | | |
|---|---|---|---|
| **B** | boug / *man, guy* | same as English | [b] |
| **Ç** | ça / *that, it's* | same as <s>; only in words *ça* and *çé* | [s] |

| | | | |
|---|---|---|---|
| **CH** | lamòché / *half* | as in English *church* | [tʃ] |
| **D** | dolo / *water* | same as English | [d] |
| **DJ** | djòb / *job* | as in English *job* | [dʒ] |
| **F** | fenm/*woman,wife* | same as English | [f] |
| **G** | gin / *to have* | as in English *game* | [g] |
| **H** | enho / *on, above* | as in English *hot* | [h] |
| **J** | jòrdi / *today* | like <*s*> in English *treasure* | [ʒ] |
| **K** | korish / *rooster* | same as English | [k] |
| **L** | las / *tired* | same as English | [l] |
| **M** | makak / *monkey* | same as English | [m] |
| **N** | nwar / *black* | same as English | [n] |
| **Ñ** | béñé / *beignet* | like <*ny*> in English *canyon* | [ɲ] |
| **P** | pær / *father* | same as English | [p] |
| **R** | rish / *rich* | flipped as in Spanish *pero* | [ɾ] |
| **S** | swété / *to wish* | same as English | [s] |
| **SH** | shar / *car* | as in English *sheep* | [ʃ] |
| **T** | ta / *a heap, a lot* | same as English | [t] |
| **V** | vré / *true* | same as English | [v] |
| **W** | wa / *to see* | same as English | [w] |
| **Y** | pyas / *dollar* | same as English | [j] |
| **Z** | zærb / *grass* | same as English | [z] |

# VOYÈL NAZAL-YÉ

Louisiana Creole, like French, has a special class of vowels that are nasalized. These vowels can create contrastive meaning in the language, unlike in English. It is difficult to describe how to nasalize a vowel, but imagine making an open vowel sound like *ah* and then slowly moving your tongue to make an <*n*> sound. Before your tongue touches the roof your mouth, the vowel sound you are making is nasalized.

The table here presents the combinations of letters used to represent nasal vowels in Louisiana Creole. The first column is the International Phonetic Alphabet (IPA) symbol for the sound. The second column shows the way(s) the sound can be written in Louisiana Creole. The third column describes the sound in terms of the vowels you have already learned above.

# SIRKOMFLÈKS-LA

The circumflex (ˆ): theoretically it can appear over any vowel, and it is used to distinguish homophones. Because there are sometimes more than two homophonous forms, however, you may need to rely on context to determine the meaning. If you see this symbol over a vowel, the vowel is pronounced exactly the same as it would be without the circumflex (except <*ê*>, which is pronounced like <*é*>).

| LETTER | DESCRIPTION | IPA |
|---|---|---|
| **an/en/am/em** | nasalized <*a*> | [ã] |
| **ònn/enn** | nasalized <*a*> followed by <*n*> | [ãn] |

| | | |
|---|---|---|
| **anm/enm** | nasalized <*a*> followed by <*m*> | [ãm] |
| **ann** | non-nasalized <*a*> followed by <*n*> | [an] |
| **amm** | non-nasalized <*a*> followed by <*m*> | [am] |
| **in/im** | nasalized <*è*> | [ɛ̃] |
| **ènn** | nasalized <*è*> followed by <*n*> | [ɛ̃n] |
| **inm** | nasalized <*è*> followed by <*m*> | [ɛ̃m] |
| **èn** | non-nasalized <*è*> followed by <*n*> | [ɛn] |
| **èm** | non-nasalized <*è*> followed by <*m*> | [ɛm] |
| **inn** | non-nasalized <*i*> followed by <*n*> | [in] |
| **imm** | non-nasalized <*i*> followed by <*m*> | [im] |
| **on/om** | nasalized <*ò*> | [ɔ̃] |
| **onn** | nasalized <*ò*> followed by <*n*> | [ɔ̃n] |
| **onm** | nasalized <*ò*> followed by <*m*> | [ɔ̃m] |
| **òn** | non-nasalized <*ò*> followed by <*n*> | [ɔn] |
| **òm** | non-nasalized <*ò*> followed by <*m*> | [ɔm] |
| **un/um** | nasalized <*œ*> | [œ̃] |
| **unn** | nasalized <*œ*> followed by <*n*> | [œ̃n] |
| **unm** | nasalized <*œ*> followed by <*m*> | [œ̃m] |
| **oun** | non-nasalized <*ou*> followed by <*n*> | [un] |
| **oum** | non-nasalized <*ou*> followed by <*m*> | [um] |
| **un** | non-nasalized <*u*> followed by <*n*> | [yn] |

# LIMIRO-YÉ

| | |
|---|---|
| **1** | ènn |
| **2** | dé |
| **3** | trò |
| **4** | kat |
| **5** | sink |
| **6** | sis |
| **7** | sèt |
| **8** | wit |
| **9** | nèf |
| **10** | dis |
| **11** | onz |
| **12** | douz |
| **13** | trèz |
| **14** | katòrz |
| **15** | kinz |
| **16** | sèz |
| **17** | dis-sèt |
| **18** | diz-wit |
| **19** | diz-nèf |
| **20** | vin |
| **21** | vint-é-ènn |
| **22** | vin-dé |
| **30** | trent |
| **40** | karant |
| **50** | sinkant |
| **60** | swasant |
| **70** | swasant-dis |
| **80** | katré-vin |
| **90** | katré-vin-dis |
| **100** | sen |
| **101** | sen ènn |
| **1000** | mil |

# Lesson 02

## *Introductions & Greetings*

Bonjou!
Bonjou!
Komen to yê?

# VOCABULARY

| | |
|---|---|
| bonjou | *hello* |
| bonswa | *good evening* |
| hé | *hey* |
| Komen to yê? | *How are you?* |
| Komen ça va? | *How's it going?* |
| Komen lê zafær? | *How are things?* |
| Ç'apé kouri? | *Is it going well?* |
| Mo pokapo(k). | *I'm OK.* |
| Mo kagou. | *I'm out of sorts.* |
| Konm-çi-konm-ça. | *OK, so-so.* |
| Mo pa byin. | *I'm not good.* |
| mærsi/mèsi | *thanks* |
| Mô nom çé... | *My name is...* |
| Ki çé tô nom? | *What is your name?* |
| Komen to pèl twa? | *What do you call yourself?* |
| Mo pèl mò... | *I call myself...* |
| Komen yé pèl twa? | *What do they call you?* |
| Yé pèl mò... | *They call me...* |
| To gin ti-nom? | *Do you have a nickname?* |
| Ki çé tô nom-d-famiy? | *What's your family name?* |
| orévwar | *goodbye* |
| Vwala... | *Here is...* |
| Mo konten fé lakònésans avèk twa. | *I'm happy to meet you.* |
| To fé lakònésans avèk...? | *Have you met... ?* |
| non (pa enkòr) | *no (not yet)* |
| wi/wé | *yes* |
| avèk/èk | *with* |

# DIALOGUE 1

A: Bonjou! Ça va?
B: Ç'apé kouri, mærsi. É twa? Komen to yê?
A: Mo byin, mærsi. Ki çé tô nom?
B: Yé pèl mò Joseph. É twa?
A: Mô nom çé Max.
B: Mo konten fé lakònésans avèk twa.
A: Parév. Orévwar!
B: Orévwar, twa!

*A: Hello! How's it going?*
*B: It's going, thanks. And you? How are you?*
*A: I'm good, thanks. What's your name?*
*B: They call me Joseph. And you?*
*A: My name is Max.*
*B: I'm happy to meet you.*
*A: Same. Goodbye!*
*B: Goodbye!*

# DIALOGUE 2

C: Hé, Louis! Komen lê zafær?
D: Konm-çi-konm-ça, mèsi.
C: To gin ti-nom?
D: Wi, mo ti-nom çé Lou.
C: Vayan! Mo pa gin ti-nom, mò.
D: Domaj.

*C: Hey, Louis! How are things?*
*D: OK, thanks.*
*C: Do you have a nickname?*
*D: Yes, my nickname is Lou.*
*C: Awesome! I don't have a nickname, me.*
*D: Too bad.*

### ★ LAGNIAPPE ★

What's your *ti-nom*? *Ti-nom* literally means 'little name', and it's not uncommon for people to be better known by this name than by the name on their birth certificate! Some *ti-nom* are based on Creole and French, others on English, and others are more creative. They can describe how someone looks, behaves, something they've done during their life, or a million other things! If you have a *ti-nom*, do you know where it comes from and what it means? If you don't, who might give you one? Get acquainted with the **Lexicon** (p. 123) at the back of this book, and see what kinds of words in there might make for a fun *ti-nom* for yourself, your friends or family!

# Lesson 03

## *Where are you from? & What do you do?*

# VOCABULARY

| | |
|---|---|
| Éyou to sòr? | *Where are you from?* |
| Ki péyi to sòr? | *What country do you come from?* |
| Dan mô famiy yé gin... | *In my family they have...* |
| Ki léta to sòr? | *What state are you from?* |
| Ki vilaj to sòr? | *What town are you from?* |
| Lavil | *New Orleans; city* |
| Mo sòr... | *I'm from...* |
| Éyou to rès astœr? | *Where do you live now?* |
| Mo rès... | *I live...* |
| résté, rès | *to live* |
| sòrti, sòr | *to be from* |
| dan lakamponñ | *in the country* |
| dan lavil | *in town* |
| a ... | *in...* |
| obòr isit | *around here* |
| o vilaj | *in the town* |
| endéyòr lavil | *outside of the city* |
| Ça to fé pou louvraj? | *What do you do for work?* |
| Ki djòb to gin/fé? | *What job do you have/do?* |
| Éyou to travay? | *Where do you work?* |
| Mo travay pa. | *I don't work.* |
| Mo travay pli. | *I don't work anymore.* |
| Mo çé étidyan. | *I'm a student.* |
| Mo fé rékòlt. | *I'm a farmer.* |
| Mo çé moun lwil. | *I'm a worker in the oil industry.* |
| Mo travay dan klo lwil. | *I work in the oilfield.* |
| Mo çé péshœr. | *I'm a fisher.* |
| Mo pèsh dê krab, dê shevrèt, dê pwason... | *I fish crabs, shrimp, fish...* |

# DIALOGUE 1

A: Éyou to sòr?
B: Mo sòr o Shikago. É twa?
A: Mo sòr o Zopélousas.
B: Ki to fé pou louvraj?
A: Mo çé moun lwil.
Mo travay dan klo lwil.
B: Mò, mo çé mèt-lékol o Nouvèl-Òrléan.

*A: Where are you from?*
*B: I'm from Chicago. And you?*
*A: I'm from Opelousas.*
*B: What do you do for work?*
*A: I work in the oil industry.*
*I work in the oilfield.*
*B: Me, I'm a teacher in New Orleans.*

# DIALOGUE 2

C: Ki çé tô louvraj?
D: Mo pa gin djòb astœr, la.
C: T'apé sharshé pou kishòj?
D: Sûr! M'olé travayé konm labitan.
C: Çé dur, do, padna.
D: Kòfær?
C: Parske çé livær — na pli louvraj jiska printem-la.
D: Shak!

*C: What's your job?*
*D: I don't have a job right now.*
*C: Are you looking for something?*
*D: Sure! I want to work as a farmer.*
*C: It's hard, though, friend.*
*D: Why?*
*C: Because it's winter — there is no more work until the spring.*
*D: Shucks!*

### ★ LAGNIAPPE ★

Take a look at the verb *sòrti, sòr.* Like many verbs, it has two forms: the long form *(sòrti)* and the short form *(sòr)*. If you're curious about this, take this as a chance to get to know the **Grammar Sketch.** Look now in the section on **Verbs** (p. 103). Don't worry if there's a lot of information, you'll figure out when to use each form over the next few lessons! Also, if you look up the verb *sòrti, sòr* in the **Lexicon** (p. 123), you'll see it has three meanings: 'to be from somewhere', 'to go out', and 'to end up'. As we head on through the book, be mindful of differences in grammar and vocabulary like these and remember to check the **Grammar Sketch** and **Lexicon** now and again.

# Lesson 04

*When is your birthday? How old are you?*

# VOCABULARY

| | |
|---|---|
| laj | *age* |
| jœn | *young* |
| vyé | *old* |
| jour | *day* |
| mwa | *month* |
| lanné | *year* |
| Kèl/ki laj to gin? | *How old are you? (literally: 'What age do you have?')* |
| Mo gin ... (zan) | *I am (have) ... years old.* |
| Kombyin zan to fé? | *How old are you turning? (literally: 'How many years do you make?)* |
| Mo fé ... zan | *I'm turning ... years old.* |
| Ki jour tô fèt? | *What day is your birthday?* |
| Çé kan tô fèt? | *When is your birthday?* |
| Mô fèt çé... | *My birthday is...* |
| Dan kèl/ki lanné to té né? | *In what year were you born?* |
| Mo té né dan... | *I was born in...* |
| Dan kèl/ki mwa to té né? | *In what month were you born?* |
| Mo té né dan mwa... | *I was born in the month...* |
| janvyé | *January* |
| févriyé | *February* |
| mars | *March* |
| avril | *April* |
| mê | *May* |
| jwin | *June* |
| jwiyèt | *July* |
| aout | *August* |
| sèptemb | *September* |
| oktòb | *October* |
| novemb | *November* |
| désemb | *December* |

# DIALOGUE 1

A: Bon fèt, Paul!
Kombyin zan to fé?
B: Mo fé kinz zan.
Kèl laj to gin, Nonk Jim?
A: Mo pli vyé ke twa;
mo gin swasant zan.
B: To byin vyé! Mo pli jœn ke twa.
Kèl jour tô fèt?
A: Mô fèt çé vint-wit mars.
B: M'a fé twa in gato pou tô fèt,
Nonk Jim!

*A: Happy birthday, Paul!*
*How old are you turning?*
*B: I'm turning fifteen.*
*How old are you, Uncle Jim?*
*A: I'm older than you;*
*I'm sixty years old.*
*B: You're real old! I'm younger than you.*
*What day is your birthday?*
*A: My birthday is the 28th of March.*
*B: I'm going to make a cake for your*
*birthday, Uncle Jim!*

# DIALOGUE 2

C: Moman, dan ki lanné to té né?
D: Mo té né dan mil-nèf-sen-sinkant.
C: Dan ki mwa?
D: Dan mwa avril.
C: Épi ki jour?
D: Sèt-la.
C: Alòr, tô fèt çé sèt avril-la?
D: Wé, é bliy pa ça!

*C: Mom, what year were you born?*
*D: I was born in 1950.*
*C: In what month?*
*D: In the month of April.*
*C: And what day?*
*D: The 7th.*
*C: So, your birthday is the 7th of April?*
*D: Yes, and don't forget it!*

**★ LAGNIAPPE ★**

The word *(l)aj* is a little special. We've written the *L* in parentheses, because it may or may not appear, and may sometimes appear as another letter. No sweat: this all depends on who you're speaking to, and using any form is acceptable! You might hear *laj, aj,* or *naj!* Capturing this incredible diversity in this book is tricky, so in the **Lexicon** you can see these words written with parentheses to show that those parts may or may not appear.

# Lesson 05

## *Family, This–That & Singular–Plural*

Famiy

# VOCABULARY

| | |
|---|---|
| moun/paren | *people, relatives* |
| mær (moman) | *mother (mom)* |
| pær (popa) | *father (dad)* |
| fenm | *woman* |
| nonm | *man* |
| Misyé | *Mister* |
| Madamm | *Ma'am* |
| fræer | *brother* |
| sœr | *sister* |
| zenfan/piti | *child* |
| fiy | *girl, daughter* |
| garçon | *boy, son* |
| gran-paren/gran-moun | *grandparents* |
| gran-mær/gran-moman | *grandmother* |
| gran-pær/gran-popa | *grandfather* |
| ti-zenfan | *grandchild* |
| ti-fiy | *granddaughter* |
| gran-ti-zenfan | *grandchild* |
| kouzin | *cousin* |
| ina | *there are* |
| kombyin | *how many* |
| Ki çé nonm-çala? | *Who is that man?* |
| Ki çé fenm-çila? | *Who is that woman?* |
| Ki moun? | *Who?* |
| bèl-mær | *mother-in-law* |
| bo-pær | *father-in-law* |
| famiy | *family* |
| -yé | *plural marker;* <br> *(see **Grammar Sketch**, p. 92)* |

# DIALOGUE 1

A: Ki moun nonm-çala?
B: Li çé mô fræer.
A: Kwa çé sô nom?
B: Sô nom çé Robert, mé sô ti-nom çé Ti-Rob.
A: Kombyin fræer to gin?
B: Mo gin ènn fræer é dé sœr. Mô fræer-yé pi résté isit.
A: Ça-fé, fenm-la çé tô sœr?
B: Non, çé mô kouzinn.

*A: Who's that man?*
*B: That's my brother.*
*A: What's his name?*
*B: His name is Robert, but his nickname is Ti-Rob.*
*A: How many brothers do you have?*
*B: I have one brother and two sisters. My brothers don't live here anymore.*
*A: So, that woman is your sister?*
*B: No, that's my cousin.*

# DIALOGUE 2

C: Kombyin moun yé gin dan tô famiy?
D: Ina sink moun: mò, mô pær, mô nonk, mô tant, é mô kouzin.
C: É tô mær?
D: Mô moman mouri trò zan pasé.
C: Ô, mo shagrin.
D: Mærsi; mò osit.

*C: How many people do you have in your family?*
*D: There are five people: me, my father, my uncle, my aunt and my cousin.*
*C: And your mother?*
*D: My mother died three years ago.*
*C: Oh, I'm sorry.*
*D: Thank you; me too.*

**⋆ LAGNIAPPE ⋆**

Try drawing a family tree. Practice the names of family members by pointing to different people and saying things like: *Li çé mô moman* / She's my Mom, or *Li çé ti-zenfan a mô popa* / He's the grandchild of my grandfather. Next, count how many family members you have: *Kombyin moun yé gin dan tô famiy?* Finally, if you label your family tree in Creole, it could make a neat poster!

# Lesson 06

## *Home, This–That & Where is it?*

# VOCABULARY

| | |
|---|---|
| lamézon | *house* |
| lakour | *yard* |
| lagalri | *porch* |
| salon | *living room* |
| sal-a-manjé | *dining room* |
| pòrt | *door* |
| mô-kin/mô-chin/mô-kènn/mô-chènn | *mine, my (emphatic)* |
| tô-kin/tô-chin/tô-kènn/tô-chènn | *yours, your (emphatic); (see* ***Grammar Sketch*** *p. 99)* |
| lakizinn | *kitchen* |
| gar-manjé | *pantry* |
| shanm | *room* |
| shanm-a-koushé | *bedroom* |
| kabinèt | *closet* |
| twalèt | *dresser* |
| shanm-bin | *bathroom* |
| komod | *toilet* |
| zétaj | *floor (of a building), story* |
| planshé | *floor* |
| lèskalyé | *stairs* |
| dê | *some (plural indefinite article)* |
| ennariyær | *behind* |
| ennavan | *in front* |
| enlè | *above, on* |
| enho | *on, above* |
| sur | *on* |
| koté | *at, near, in place of* |
| apré | *after* |
| dési | *on top, over* |
| enba | *below, under* |

## DIALOGUE 1

A: Kombyin shanm ina dan tô lamézon?

B: Ina lakizinn, dé shanm-a-koushé, salon-la, é ina ènn shanm-a-bin. Ça fé yé gin sink shanm. É tô-chin?

A: Mô-chin gin sèt shanm: lakizinn, dé shanm-a-binn, dé shanm-a-koushé, salon-la é in lakav.

B: Tô lakav enba?

A: Wi.

B: No pe pa gin lakav enba o Nouvèl-Òrléan. Ina tro dolo. To gin lashans, twa.

A: Petèt, mé vouzòt rès dan Lalwizyann é mo rès dan Indiana. Ça fé vouzòt gin lashans!

B: Hm. To gin rézon, la.

A: *How many rooms are there in your house?*

B: *There is the kitchen, two bedrooms, the living room, and a bathroom. So, they have six rooms. And yours?*

A: *My house has seven rooms: the kitchen, two bathrooms, two bedrooms, the living room and a basement.*

B: *Is your basement underneath?*

A: *Yes.*

B: *We can't have basements underneath in New Orleans. There's too much water. You're lucky, you.*

A: *Maybe, but y'all live in Louisiana and I live in Indiana. Y'all are lucky!*

B: *Hm. You're right about that.*

# DIALOGUE 2

C: Mo bezwin komod-la! Éyou li yê?
D: Li enho lèskalyé. Dèzyèm zétaj-la.
C: OK, mærsi!
D: Pa-d-kwa.
C: Byin, byin mærsi; mo mank èksplozé!
D: Çé pa aryin, mé fé vit, la!
Ç'alé sòrti salé si to fé pipi sur planshé mô gran-mær.

*C: I need the toilet! Where is it?*
*D: It's up the stairs. The second floor.*
*C: OK, thanks!*
*D: You're welcome.*
*C: Thanks so much; I'm almost exploding!*
*D: It's nothing, but be quick!*
*It's going to end up badly if you pee on my grandmother's floor.*

**★ LAGNIAPPE ★**

Check out the use of the verb *manké, mank* in Dialogue 2. Usually, it means 'to miss': *Mo mank twa* / I miss you; *Mo manké bòs-la* / I missed the bus. Here, it has another meaning: 'to almost do something'. *To manké manké ça, non?!* / You almost missed that, huh?!

Another thing you might have missed is the name of 'New Orleans' in Creole — this can be *Nouvèl-Òrléan*, or, more commonly, just *Lavil*, which just means 'The City'.

# Lesson 07

## *Weather & Outdoors*

# VOCABULARY

| | |
|---|---|
| déyòr | *outside* |
| Komen tem-la yê? | *How's the weather?* |
| montañ | *mountain* |
| pléri | *prairie* |
| plènn | *plain* |
| sipriyær | *swamp, cypress swamp* |
| péyi-ba | *forest, swamp, wetland* |
| dibwa | *wood, woods* |
| lariviyær | *river* |
| narb | *tree* |
| zærb | *grass* |
| labou | *mud* |
| lamær | *sea* |
| bayou | *bayou* |
| flœr | *flower* |
| Soléy-la apé briyé. | *The sun is shining.* |
| Lapli apé tombé. | *The rain is falling.* |
| Ç'apé mouyé. | *It's raining.* |
| Diven-la apé souflé. | *The wind is blowing.* |
| Ina movétem/gro tem. | *There is bad weather.* |
| Tònær apé gronyin. | *Thunder is rumbling.* |
| zéklær | *lightning* |
| Li fé fré/frèt. | *It's cold.* |
| Li fé sho. | *It's hot.* |
| Li fé bo; Çé bo; Gin bo tem. | *The weather is good.* |
| Si tem-la jlé, yé va gin laglas. | *If it's freezing, there will be ice.* |
| kouvær | *cloudy* |
| Ina in ta nwaj dan syèl-la. | *There's a lot of clouds in the sky.* |

# DIALOGUE 1

A: Komen tem-la jòrdi?
B: Li mòyær kouvær; ina bokou nwaj.
A: Li fé fré?
B: Non, li fé bo.
T'olé kouri o park?
A: Petèt. Ça senm lapli?
B: Mo pa konné, mé mo kròpa.
To pens t'a fonn si to mouyé?
A: Non, shær, mé mo p'olé barbouyé mô nouvo bòt-yé!
B: Byin, kòfær to ashté bòt si yé pe pa marshé dan labou?

*A: How is the weather?*
*B: It's quite cloudy; there's a lot of clouds.*
*A: Is it cold?*
*B: No, the weather is good.*
*Do you want to go to the park?*
*A: Maybe. Does it seem like it will rain?*
*B: I don't know, I don't think so.*
*Do you think you'll melt if you're wet?*
*A: No, cher, but I don't want to get my new boots dirty!*
*B: Well, why did you buy the boots if they can't walk in mud?*

# DIALOGUE 2

C: Ki kalité plant yé gin dan lakour?
D: Tou kalité. Ina dê narb, dê flœr, dê zærb, toukishòj.
C: Moun ka manjé ça?
D: Zen dê plant to ka manjé; no sær féy sasafra pou fé lapoud filé é no mèt ça dan gombo. Li gou bon!

*C: What kind of plants do they have in the yard?*
*D: All kinds. There are trees, flowers, grass, everything.*
*C: Can people eat that?*
*D: There are plants you can eat; we use sassafras leaves to make filé powder and we put it in gumbo. It tastes good!*

**★ LAGNIAPPE ★**

Look at the two different words for 'can' used in the dialogues: *yé pe pa marshé dan labou* / they can't walk in mud (Dialogue 1); *dê plant to ka manjé* / plants you can eat (Dialogue 2). These two words *pe* and *ka(pab)* can be used interchangeably, usage which differs in different regions. It's also important to remember how to use these words in the correct order. Check out the different position of *pa* in these two sentences: *to pa ka manjé* / you can't eat, but *to pe pa manjé* / you can't eat. Make sure you check the **Grammar Sketch** section on **Preverbal Markers** (p. 105) to learn more about important little words like these.

# Lesson 08

## *Time, Routines, School–Work & Past*

Va Wa Kèl lœn

# VOCABULARY

| | |
|---|---|
| Kèl/Ki lœr li yê? | *What time is it?* |
| a ... œr | *at ... o'clock* |
| (É)kan? | *When?* |
| Kèl/Ki jour? | *What day?* |
| souven | *often* |
| toultem | *always* |
| touléjour | *everyday* |
| té | *past marker;* |
| | *(see **Grammar Sketch**, p. 108)* |
| défwa | *sometimes* |
| byin rar | *rarely* |
| jamé | *never* |
| en jénéral | *in general* |
| lékòl | *school* |
| lofis | *office* |
| travayé, travay | *to work* |
| lindi | *Monday* |
| mardi | *Tuesday* |
| mærkrédi | *Wednesday* |
| jédi | *Thursday* |
| vendrédi | *Friday* |
| sanmdi | *Saturday* |
| dimansh | *Sunday* |

# DIALOGUE 1

A: Kèl lœr vouzòt kouri lékòl?
B: No kouri lékòl a wit œr shak matin.
A: Çé bonnœr! Mo té konné kouri lékòl a nèf œr. É kan zòt vyin bæk lamézon?
B: No kit lékòl a trò zœr, no èspær bòs-la, é no vyin bæk lamézon a trò zœr é demi.

*A: What time do y'all go to school?*
*B: We go to school at eight o'clock every morning.*
*A: That's early! I used to go to school at nine o'clock. And when do you come home?*
*B: We leave school at three o'clock, we wait for the bus, and we come back home at half past three.*

# DIALOGUE 2

C: Ki jour to fé tô ménaj?
D: En jénéral mo fé mô ménaj pendan fin-lasmènn. É twa?
C: Çé byin rar mo fé mô-chin ménaj. Mo mand mô bèl pou fé li.
D: Vilin! Kòfær to fé ça?
C: Mé mo travay pendan tou lasmènn!
D: É li-minm?
C: Wé... li travay osit...
D: Alòr senm to gin pou édé li èk ménaj-la.

*C: What day do you do your chores?*
*D: In general I do my chores on the weekend. And you?*
*C: I hardly ever do my own chores. I ask my girlfriend to do it.*
*D: That's mean! Why do you do that?*
*C: But I work all week!*
*D: And her?*
*C: Yeah... She works too...*
*D: Well it seems like you have to help her out with the chores.*

**★ LAGNIAPPE ★**

Many Creole routines and traditions formed according to the Catholic calendar. Before retiring for the evening, families would gather together to pray with their *shaplé* / rosary beads. For *La Tou-Sin* / All Saints' Day, the community would gather to *blanshi* / whitewash the graves of their loved ones. Today, it is common to see *krébis* / crawfish being boiled on *Vendrédi Sin* / Good Friday. And, of course there is *Mardi Gra*, the well-known celebration before *Mærkrédi dê Senn* / Ash Wednesday and the start of *Karèm* / Lent. Perhaps *Madanm Grand Dwa* / Lady Long Fingers or *Ti Nonm Janviyé* / Little Man January placed fruit and trinkets in your Christmas or New Year's Day stocking? *Ki dòt tradisyon to konné?* / What other traditions can you think of?

# Lesson 09

## *Likes–Dislikes & Hobbies*

Mo linm tua
kom ti
koshon linm
labou

# VOCABULARY

| | |
|---|---|
| Ça to linm fé? | *What do you like to do?* |
| Mo linm... | *I like...* |
| Mo linm pa... | *I don't like...;* *(see **Grammar Sketch**, p. 96)* |
| linmé, linm | *to like; to love* |
| ékri | *to write* |
| fé lashas | *to hunt* |
| shasé, shas | *to hunt* |
| lir, li | *to read* |
| jwé, jou | *to play* |
| kouté lamizik | *to listen to music* |
| gété pòrtré | *to watch a movie* |
| galopé, galòp | *to run* |
| monté shval | *to ride a horse* |
| péshé, pèsh | *to fish* |
| monté bisik | *to ride a bike* |
| najé, naj | *to swim* |
| Asit prenn lafrèsh en lagalri. | *Taking the air on the porch.* |

## ⋆ LAGNIAPPE ⋆

One hobby we didn't mention: learning Creole! *To linm aprenn Kréyòl? No swèt to linm ça!* You're now halfway through the book: *bon djòb!* You're now also one of many people who are working hard to reclaim and revitalize the Louisiana Creole language. In the back of this book, you'll find a section called **More Resources** (p. 166) — here you can find places to practice what you've learned, ask questions and join the community of people learning and speaking every day. Come join us!

# DIALOGUE 1

A: John, ça to linm fé kan
to travay pa?
B: Mo linm bwa labyær é asit prenn
lafrèsh en lagalri.
A: Ça senm bon.
To kout lamizik?
B: Wi, mo linm ça osit.
Zen dê fwa mo kout lamizik tandi
m'apé asit en lagalri.
A: Mo linm péshé kan mo gin tem.
B: Ki kalité pwason to linm trapé?
A: Mo linm trapé dê patasa parske
yé gou bon.
Mo linm pa tro pwason-armé, la.
B: Proshin fwa to trap in pwason-armé,
mènn mò ça!

*A: John, what do you like to do when
you don't work?*
*B: I like to drink beer and take
the air on the porch.*
*A: That sounds good.
Do you listen to music?*
*B: Yes, I like that too.
Sometimes I listen to music while
I'm sitting on the porch.*
*A: I like to fish when I have time.*
*B: What kind of fish do you like to catch?*
*A: I like to catch sunfish because
they taste good.
I don't like gar too much.*
*B: Next time you catch a gar,
bring it to me!*

# DIALOGUE 2

C: OK, mô fiy, ça t'olé fé?
T'olé monté bisik?
D: Non!
C: T'olé kouri najé?
D: Non!
C: Alòr, ça ina èk twa?
D: To promèt pou ménné mò gété
"The Princess and the Frog"!
To fé særmen!

*C: OK, my girl, what do you want to do?
Do you want to ride your bike?*
*D: No!*
*C: Do you want to go swimming?*
*D: No!*
*C: So what's up with you?*
*D: You promised to take me to watch
"The Princess and the Frog"!
You swore you would!*

# Lesson 10

## *Clothes & Body Parts*

# VOCABULARY

| | |
|---|---|
| Mo mèt... | *I put on...* |
| latèt | *head* |
| shévé | *hair* |
| laboush | *mouth* |
| né | *nose* |
| lalanng | *tongue* |
| den | *teeth* |
| zòrèy | *ear* |
| zyè | *eye* |
| kou | *neck* |
| bra | *arm* |
| lamin | *hand* |
| dwa | *finger* |
| lèstoma | *stomach* |
| janmb | *leg* |
| pyé | *foot* |
| zòrtèy | *toe* |
| shapo | *hat* |
| shimiz | *shirt* |
| sinturon | *belt* |
| kalçon | *underwear* |
| kilot | *pants* |
| linèt | *glasses* |
| soulyé | *shoe* |
| bòt | *boot* |
| ròb | *robe* |
| lajup | *skirt* |
| sandal | *sandals* |
| jozé | *blouse* |
| jakèt | *jacket* |
| kapo léjé/lour | *light/heavy coat* |
| kilot kout | *shorts* |

# DIALOGUE 1

A: Ki ça to mèt kan li fé
fré déyòr?
B: Mo mèt shapo, jakèt, kilot,
èk in pær bòt.
A: Ékan tem-la bo?
B: La, mo ot tou ça é mo mèt mô
kilot kout, in T-shirt, é mô sandal-yé.
A: Mo linm pa pòrté sandal akòz
mô pyé-yé vini barbouyé.
B: Alòr, marsh pa dan labou, padna.

*A: What do you wear when it's
cold outside?*
*B: I wear a hat, jacket, pants
and a pair of boots.*
*A: And when the weather is nice?*
*B: Then, I take all that off and put on
short pants, a t-shirt, and my sandals.*
*A: I don't like to wear sandals because
my feet get dirty.*
*B: Well then don't walk in the mud, friend.*

# DIALOGUE 2

C: To gin in joli lajup la!
Mo linm koulœr-la.
D: Mèsi! Mo linm koulœr
tô ròb la osit.
C: T'olé mo édé twa oté
tô jakèt?
D: O, byin mærsi, mô fiy.
Éyou tô-chin jakèt?
C: Mo pa pòrté jakèt jòrdi, moman.
D: To va trapé in larimm!

*C: You have a pretty skirt there!*
*I love the color.*
*D: Thanks! I love the color of*
*your dress too.*
*C: Do you want me to help you take*
*your jacket off?*
*D: Oh, thanks a lot, my girl.*
*Where's your own jacket?*
*C: I wasn't wearing a jacket today, mom.*
*D: You're going to catch a cold!*

**★ LAGNIAPPE ★**

Did you know it is bad luck to store your *soulyé* above your *latèt?* Have you ever gotten a bump on the tip of your *lalanng?* That means you lied about something. You definitely don't want to throw the *shévé* from your comb outside because if a bird makes a nest out of it, you will have a *mal-dé-tèt* / headache for the rest of your life. And, if your *né* itches, don't answer that door because an old man is coming to your house to kiss you. Superstitions are embedded in Louisiana Creole culture and language. Superstitions as well as proverbs guide one's life and help to keep one safe from dangers, real and imagined. Sometimes, proverbs can best be understood in their original language. Learning the language is the best way to understand the culture of a people.

# Lesson 11

## *Health, Sickness, Injury & Reflexive Verbs*

# VOCABULARY

| | |
|---|---|
| Mo sen mò(-minm)... | *I feel...* |
| byin | *good* |
| malad | *sick* |
| Ki fé mal? | *What hurts?* |
| Mô ... fé mal | *My ... hurts.* |
| Mo gin mal... | *I have ...ache* |
| tousé, tous | *to cough* |
| étærné, étærn | *to sneeze* |
| mal-latèt/mal-de-tèt | *headache* |
| mal-o-do | *backache* |
| mal-zòrèy | *earache* |
| mal-o-vant/mal-lèstoma | *stomach ache* |
| mal-lagòrj/mal-de-gòrj | *sore throat* |
| réshté, réshèt | *vomit* |
| tous | *cough* |
| (la)chirout | *diarrhea* |
| gayar | *healthy* |

# DIALOGUE 1

A: Ça ina?
B: Mo sen pa mò tro byin.
A: Ki çé ça ki fé mal?
B: Mô lèstoma fé mal;
mo gin mal-lèstoma.
A: Ki ça to manjé yær?
B: Mo pa konné... enlentour kinz
liv krébis?

*A: What's up?*
*B: I don't feel too good.*
*A: What's hurting?*
*B: My stomach hurts;*
*I have a stomach ache.*
*A: What did you eat yesterday?*
*B: I don't know... around fifteen*
*pounds of crawfish?*

## DIALOGUE 2

C: Senm to malad ojòrdi!
D: Wi, mo t'apé tousé épi étærné dépi bonnœr matin-çila.
C: Prenn latizann avèk dimyèl. Ça va édé twa.
D: Mærsi, m'a fé ça talœr.
C: Mèt kèk féy dibonm endan li.
D: OK, mo gin dité kammòmèl shé mò.

*C: It seems you're sick today!*
*D: Yes, I've been coughing and sneezing since early this morning.*
*C: Take herbal tea with milk. That will help you.*
*D: Thanks, I'll do that later.*
*C: Put some mint leaves in it.*
*D: OK, I have some chamomile tea at my place.*

### ⋆ LAGNIAPPE ⋆

*To konné ki çé in trétœr? Çé in moun ki trèt moun malad.* / Have you ever heard of a traiteur? It's a person who 'treats' / *trété, trèt* sick people. Traiteurs practice traditional medicine, which centres around specific prayers, and might also involve laying on hands, a herbal remedy / *réméd*, or even something more elaborate like tying strings or burying something in the yard at a certain time. If you head on down the bayou and ask around, you'll definitely find someone who can treat warts, sunstroke, eczema, arthritis and more... *Ça to krò?* Here's a secret: *ènn dan moun ki ékri Ti Liv-la té kouri wa in trétœr pou movè lapo... épi sô movè lapo jamé vini bæk!*

# Lesson 12

## *Invitations, Questions & Excuses*

Vouzòt pyinvini
pasé kote
nou!

## VOCABULARY

| | |
|---|---|
| Vyin... | *Come...* |
| T'olé vini...? | *Do you want to come...?* |
| Ki/kèl lœr? | *What time?* |
| Ki/kèl jour? | *What day?* |
| Kòfær?? | *Why?* |
| Mo sé linmé, mé... | *I'd like to, but...* |
| Mo pa kapab parske... | *I can't because...* |
| Mo pe pa parske... | *I can't because...* |
| pòrtré | *movie; picture* |
| Ça senm/gin lè... | *It seems like...* |
| dwa | *ought* |
| gin pou | *have to* |
| aswa | *tonight* |
| kité, kit | *to leave* |
| lésé trankil | *to leave alone* |

## DIALOGUE 1

A: Hé! Vyin gété in pòrtré avèk nouzòt aswa.
B: Mo sé linmé, mé mô tèt fé mal.
A: Kòfær to jamé olé sòrti èk nou?
B: Mo pe pa gété pòrtré kan mo gin in tèl mal-latèt.
A: Gin lè to linm pa gin bon tem.
B: Çé pa ça, mo jish sen mò in ti brin malad. In nòt fwa, zami.

*A: Hey! Come watch a movie with us tonight.*
*B: I'd love to, but my head hurts.*
*A: Why do you never want to come out with us?*
*B: I can't watch a movie when I have a headache.*
*A: Seems like you don't like to have a good time.*
*B: It's not that, I just feel a little sick. Another time, friend.*

# DIALOGUE 2

C: Bonswa, boug!
No va fé sosyété démin oswa.
T'olé vini?
D: Ki lœr?
C: Ora wit lœr.
D: Éyou?
C: Lamézon mô paren-yé.
Yé gin bokou plas pou toukèkènn.
D: Dakòr, mo va dèt la. Mærsi!

*C: Good evening, dude! We're going to throw a party tomorrow evening. Do you want to come?*
*D: What time?*
*C: Around eight o'clock.*
*D: Where?*
*C: My parents' house. They have a lot of space for everyone.*
*D: OK, I'll be there. Thanks!*

**★ LAGNIAPPE ★**

Kouri-Vini did not just stay in Louisiana. Natural disasters such as The Great Mississippi Flood of 1927 combined with the Great Depression were two reasons people moved out of Louisiana en masse. They moved west, from Texas to California, and they moved north along the Mississippi to places like St. Louis and Chicago. As Louisiana Creoles migrated, they took their culture and language with them. That is why, though increasingly rare, you may still find people in the Louisiana Diaspora who have kept the language in their families. Do you live in the diaspora and want to reconnect with one of our heritage languages? Keep using this book and then see **More Resources** (p. 166).

# Lesson 13

## *Travel, Directions & Future*

# VOCABULARY

| | |
|---|---|
| Éyou t'apé kouri? | *Where are you going?* |
| Mo va... | *I'm going...* |
| M'alé... | *I'm going...* |
| drwa | *right* |
| gosh | *left* |
| tòrné, tòrn | *turn* |
| kontiné | *continue* |
| rodayé, roday | *to travel on the road, roam, gallivant* |
| galope chmen-yé | *to run the road* |
| vwayajé, vwayaj | *to travel* |
| Bon vwayaj! | *Have a good trip!* |
| sto | *store* |
| lagrosri | *grocery store* |
| boutik | *store* |
| prenn | *to take* |
| trin | *train* |
| shar | *car* |
| éroplènn | *airplane* |
| bato | *boat* |

# DIALOGUE 1

A: Éyou t'apé kouri?
B: M'ap kouri a lagrosri, mé mo pærdi.
A: Pou arivé a lagrosri, kontiné dé mil épi tòrn a gosh kan to wa gro sipré-la. Swiv shmin-çala jiska lagrosri la. Di Misyé Charlot bonjou pou sô zami Freddy.
B: Byin mærsi!

*A: Where are you going?*
*B: I'm going to the grocery store, but I'm lost.*
*A: To get to the grocery store, continue two miles and then turn left when you see the big cedar. Follow that road until the grocery store. Tell Mister Charlot hello from his friend Freddy.*
*B: Thanks a lot!*

## DIALOGUE 2

C: Ki ça vouzòt apé fé pendan lété?
D: No va rodayé jiska Kanada.
C: Ça yé gin laba?
D: Yé gin in ta pou wa é fé. Lavil Montréal gin in gro fèt lamizik djaz, ina bokou park nasyonal, é toukishòj.
C: Mé tem-la fé fré laba, wi?
D: Pa dan lété. Li byin bo.
C: Alòr kombyin jour vou bezwin pou kouri la?
D: N'a prenn trò kat jour.

*C: What are you going to do during the summer?*
*D: We're going to take a road trip to Canada.*
*C: What do they have over there?*
*D: They have a lot to see and do. The city of Montreal has a big jazz music festival, there are a lot of national parks, and everything.*
*C: But the weather is cold over there, yeah?*
*D: Not in the summer. It's really nice.*
*C: So how many days do y'all need to get there?*
*D: We're taking three or four days.*

### ★ LAGNIAPPE ★

Louisiana Creole is a special language, deeply steeped in the story of the diverse populations who make up the Gulf South. But did you know that there are French-based creole languages spoken on at least five continents? Each of these languages is unique and not everyone can understand everyone else, but they all also have things in common. All through the Caribbean, to the Indian Ocean, to the streets of Paris, France or the beaches of Miami, Florida... if you listen hard enough, you might just find yourself hearing some familiar sounds...

# Lesson 14

## *If–Then*

# VOCABULARY

| | |
|---|---|
| Si to..., to sé... | *If you..., you would ...* |
| Si to..., to sa... | *If you..., you will ...* |
| Si to travay tro, to sé/sa las. | *If you work too much, you would be/will be tired.* |
| Si mo té gin asé larjen, mo sé fé li ranjé shar-la. | *If I had had enough money, I would have had him fix the car.* |
| Si yé vyin aswa, li sé kwi soupé pou yé. | *If they come this evening, he will cook dinner for them.* |
| lis | *list* |
| ganñé, ganñ | *win* |
| (la)lotri | *lottery* |
| (la)shas | *hunt* |
| shasé, shas | *to hunt* |

# DIALOGUE 1

A: Yéyay, mo gin in ta pou fé démin! Mo gin pou kouri a Lafayèt pou ashté kèk nouvo linj pou mô piti. Apré ça, m'ap kouri war mô bèl-sœr a Sésilya. Apré ça, mo stil gin pou fé grosri...

B: Mé mò, mo gin pou kouri o sto démin itou. Si to di mò ça to bezwin, m'alé ashté kèk zafær pou twa.

A: Mé ça çé vayan, shær! Gèt, ça çé mô lis. Si to ashèt tou ça, mo sa bokou konten!

B: Oké, alon wa... mé, shær, to ékri in ta zafær isit!

A: Wèl, si mo ashèt pa in ta, no va pa gin asé pou manjé. Çé lafèt mô garçon é tou la famiy vyin manjé shé nouzòt!

B: Si mo té konné ça, mo sé pa di ariyin!

A: *Yeyay, I have a ton to do tomorrow! I have to go to Lafayette to buy some new clothes for my children. After that, I'm going to see my sister-in-law in Cecilia. After that, I still have to go make groceries...*

B: *But me, I have to go to the store tomorrow too. If you tell me what you need, I'll buy some things for you.*

A: *But that's real nice of you! Look, this is my list. If you buy all that, I'll be really happy!*

B: *OK, let's see... but, cher, you wrote a whole bunch of stuff here!*

A: *Well, if I don't buy a whole bunch, we won't have enough to eat. It's my son's birthday and all the family are coming to our place!*

B: *If I had known that, I wouldn't have said anything!*

# DIALOGUE 2

C: Ça to sé fé si to sé ganñé lalotri?
D: Mò, mo sé kité mô djòb, bati mò in nouvo mézon dan la kamponñ, épi résté la tousœl.
C: Mé si to rès laba tousœl, to sa ennwiyé!
D: Mo p'olé pærsonn vini embarasé mò pou mô larjen. Ça-fé mo sé kouri résté obòr bayou laba la éyou mô ti frèr fé lashas.
C: Laba, la? Wé, mo konné! Si to ganñ lalotri é to gonn laba, m'a vini vizité!
D: Mé to kanay, twa!

*C: What would you do if you won the lottery?*
*D: Me, I'd leave my job, build myself a new house in the country, and live all alone.*
*C: But if you live there all alone, you'll be bored!*
*D: I don't want anyone to come and bother me for my money. So I'd go and live by the bayou there where my little brother goes hunting.*
*C: Down there? Yeah, I know! If you win the lottery and you go down there, I'll come visit!*
*D: You're sly, you!*

**★ LAGNIAPPE ★**

Today Louisiana Creole speakers can be found in many different places, but historically they have been concentrated in a few areas throughout the state of Louisiana: in communities along Bayou Teche, on the northshore of Lake Pontchartrain, in the area known as the German Coast (upriver from New Orleans, downriver from Baton Rouge), Pointe Coupee Parish, within New Orleans, and around Natchitoches. The language is also spoken in diaspora communities in Texas, California, Illinois, and elsewhere.

# Lesson 15

## *Music, Church, Dancehall & Courting*

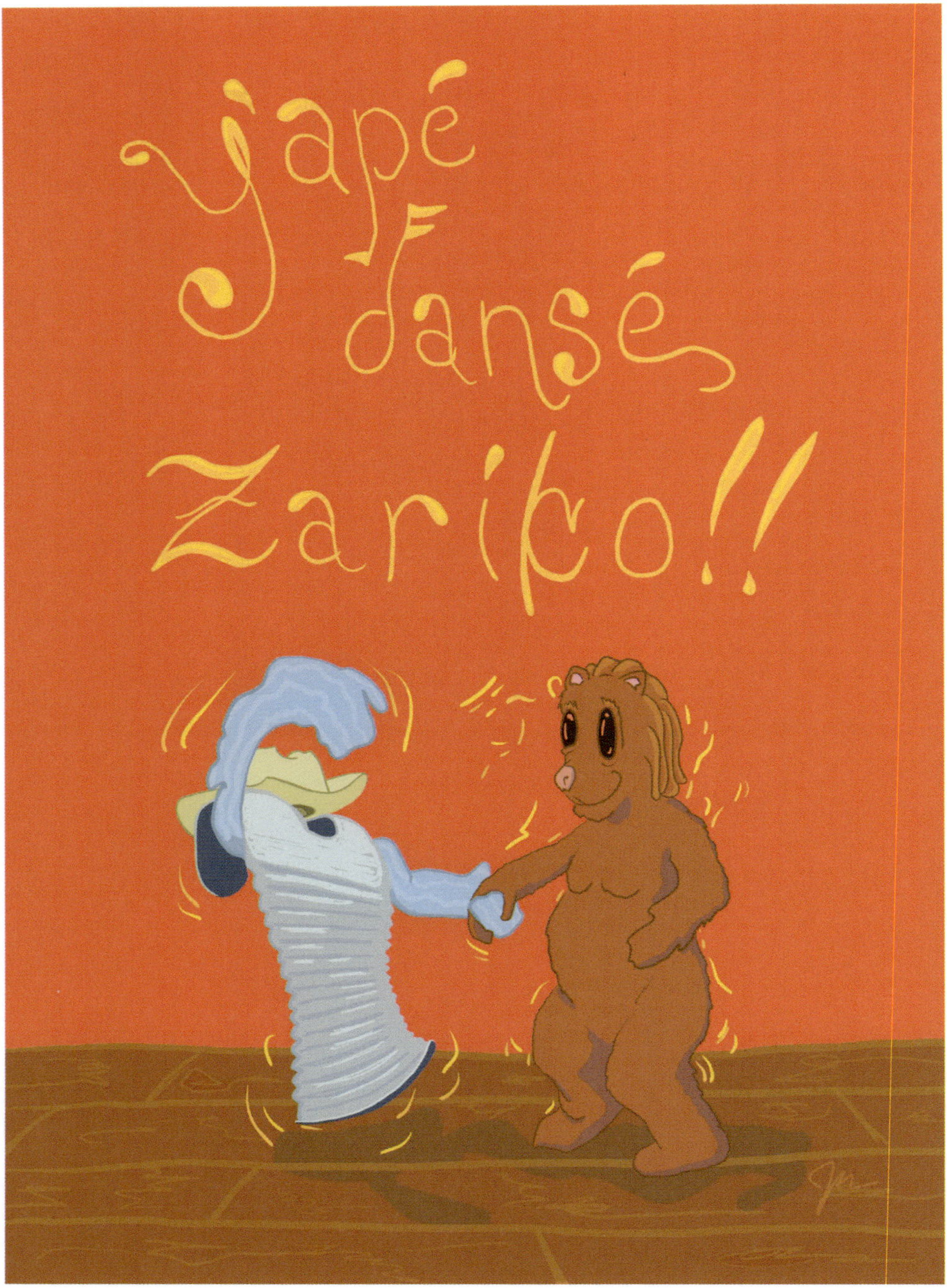
Yapé
Fanse
Zariko!!

# VOCABULARY

| | |
|---|---|
| lamizik | *music* |
| légliz | *church* |
| hòl | *hall* |
| klœb | *club* |
| bal | *ball* |
| shanté, shant | *to sing* |
| dansé, dans | *to dance* |
| jwé, jou | *to play* |
| spìnn | *to spin records* |
| fé lamour | *to court* |
| fé lakour | *to date* |
| fèt | *party* |
| fé sosyété | *to throw a party* |
| mariyé | *to marry* |
| fiyansé | *to be engaged* |
| koundjay | *(a type of dance)* |
| vals | *waltz* |
| zariko | *zydeco* |
| gita | *guitar* |
| tambou | *drum* |
| (la)vyolon | *violin* |

# DIALOGUE 1

A: Ki ça k'apé dansé avèk Marie, la?
B: Çé mô kouzin, Billy. Senm l'ap fé lakour apré ti fiy-çala.
A: Yé pe dansé bokou byin!
B: Lamizik isit çé vayan aswa, la.

*A: Who's that dancing with Marie, there?*
*B: That's my cousin, Billy. Seems like he's dating that girl there.*
*A: They can dance really well!*
*B: The music here is awesome tonight.*

## DIALOGUE 2

C: Kèk moun légliz va fé sosyété pou fèt mô moman. T'olé vini èk mò?
D: Yé va gin lamizik?
C: O, wi! Nora lamizik, manjé, divin, tou ça.
D: No va dansé ensenm?
C: Si t'olé, shær!
D: Mo jamé kouri in fèt san dansé.

*C: Some people from church are going to throw a party for my mother's birthday. Do you want to come with me?*
*D: Will they have music?*
*C: Oh, yes! There will be music, food, wine, all that.*
*D: Are we going to dance together?*
*C: If you want, cher!*
*D: I never go to a party without dancing.*

### ⋆ LAGNIAPPE ⋆

You might be surprised to learn that the word 'zydeco' actually comes from the Creole word, *zariko*. And one of the most popular phrases in zydeco songs is still *Lê zariko yé pa salé* / The snap beans aren't salty. This expression was used as a way to say that times are hard. Normally a family would season their snap beans with a piece of tasso or bacon, so if the snap beans weren't salty, that meant there hadn't been enough money for the meat. *Ça çé dur, padna!*

# Lesson 16

## *Farming, Garden & Animals*

Li t'apé fé jardinaj kan li té wa in wawaron

# VOCABULARY

| | |
|---|---|
| jardinaj | *vegetables* |
| grènn | *seed* |
| margo | *starter potato/plant* |
| fimyé | *manure, fertilizer* |
| rashé, rash | *to pull out* |
| jardin | *garden* |
| sinmé, sinm | *to sow* |
| tòrné latær | *to till* |
| rékòlt | *harvest, crop* |
| bité , bit | *to mound, heap up (soil)* |
| mayi | *corn* |
| diri | *rice* |
| dékònn | *sugarcane* |
| zònyon | *onion* |
| déshou | *cabbage* |
| poul | *chicken, hen* |
| pintal | *guinea fowl* |
| zèf | *egg* |
| nik | *nest* |
| vash | *cow* |
| koshon faroush | *boar, wild pig* |
| fid | *feed* |
| difwin | *hay* |
| lapay | *straw* |
| shévréy | *deer* |
| wawaron | *bullfrog* |
| lavyònn | *meat* |

# DIALOGUE 1

A: Ça yé konné fé pendan in laboushri?
B: Yé chou kèk koshon, é yé fé toukishòj avèk li. Boudin, landoui, toukishòj konm ça.
A: Çé tou?
B: Wi, é tem-zen-tem ina lamizik.
A: Yé chou bèf osit?
B: Wi, mé pa en minm tem.

*A: What do they usually do during a boucherie?*
*B: They kill some pigs, and they'd make all kinds of stuff with it. Boudin, andouille, all kinds of stuff like that.*
*A: That's all?*
*B: Yes, and sometimes there's music.*
*A: Do they kill cattle too?*
*B: Yes, but not at the same time.*

# DIALOGUE 2

C: Mô gran-mær planté sô jardin yær matin.
D: Kwa li planté?
C: Li planté ti margo patat anglèz, patat dous, zònyon, tomat, mayi taktak...
D: Mo linm taktak! Ékan li va dèt paré?
C: Ifo spéré, padna. Ça ka prenn kèk mwa.
D: Kèk mwa? Non. M'ap kouri lagrosri ashté mô-chin taktak, mèsi bokou.

*C: My grandma planted her garden yesterday morning.*
*D: What did she plant?*
*C: She planted starters for English potatoes, sweet potatoes, onions, tomatoes, popcorn...*
*D: I love popcorn! When will it be ready?*
*C: You have to wait, buddy. We have to wait a few months.*
*D: A few months? No. I'm going to the grocery store and buying my own popcorn, thank you very much.*

**★ LAGNIAPPE ★**

Louisiana Creole and Louisiana French have a very close relationship. In fact, many native speakers will use one word (either *French* or *Creole*) to describe all the French-based language varieties of the Gulf South. Believe it or not, a speaker of Louisiana French (some speakers call this *Cajun French*), will probably have an easier time understanding Louisiana Creole than Parisian French. This remarkable fact highlights the deeply intertwined histories of the region's languages and its peoples.

# Lesson 17

## *Cooking, Food & Adjectives*

Zòt Paré
pou manjé
digonbo zèb?

# VOCABULARY

| | |
|---|---|
| déjœné, déjœn | *to have breakfast* |
| dinné, dinn | *to have lunch* |
| soupé, soup | *to have dinner* |
| myété, myèt | *to snack* |
| manjé, manj | *to eat* |
| bwason | *drink* |
| bwa | *to drink* |
| kwi | *to cook* |
| bouyi, bouy | *to boil* |
| brilé, bril | *to burn* |
| frikasé | *fricasee, stew; to stew* |
| griyé, griy | *to grill* |
| roti | *to roast* |
| stov | *stove* |
| kru | *raw* |
| boukònné, boukònn | *to smoke* |
| pla | *plate, dish (of food)* |
| bòl | *bowl* |
| kiyær | *spoon* |
| kouto | *knife* |
| fourshèt | *fork* |
| tas/kòp | *cup* |
| vær | *glass* |
| dou | *sweet* |
| anmær | *bitter* |
| salé | *salty* |
| fad | *bland* |
| sézonné, sézonn | *to season* |
| pimenté | *spicy* |
| frèsh | *fresh* |
| shodyær | *pot* |

# DIALOGUE 1

A: To linm tô manjé byin sézonné?
B: Wé, mèt bokou pimen é zépis endan li.
A: To jamé manjé dan Lalwizyann.
B: Non, kòfær?
A: Ariyin. Vwala tô gombo.
B: KO! Çé difé la!
A: Mo séyé di twa...
B: Dolo! Vit!

*A: Do you like your food well seasoned?*
*B: Yes, put a lot of pepper and spice in there.*
*A: You've never eaten in Louisiana.*
*B: No, why?*
*A: Nothing. Here's your gumbo.*
*B: KO! It's fire!*
*A: I tried to tell you...*
*B: Water! Quick!*

# DIALOGUE 2

C: Komen to kwi lê zariko?
D: Mo mèt yé dan dolo aswa avan m'olé kwi yé. La, mo fé yé bouyi épi konsommé pendan kèk lœr.
C: To mèt ça avèk diri?
D: Wé! To pe pa manjé zariko san diri.

*C: How do you cook your green beans?*
*D: I put them in water the evening before I cook them. Then I boil them and then eat them within a few hours.*
*C: Do you put them with rice?*
*D: Yes! You can't eat beans without rice.*

### ★ LAGNIAPPE ★

The word *brulé* is included in the following traditional Creole song: *Sot krapo tô ké va brilé. Prenn kouraj. Li va répousé.* / Jump frog, your tail will burn. Take courage, it will grow again. In Louisiana Creole culture, there are traditional folk songs in French, Spanish, and Kouri-Vini. A few of these songs were written and recorded. Other songs were simply told orally from generation to generation. Oral storytelling is another Louisiana Creole tradition. Many of these oral stories came to Louisiana by way of enslaved people from Africa. Have you ever heard the stories of *Kompær Lapin and Kompær Bouki*? The smart Lapin and his gullible friend Bouki will certainly make you laugh. Be sure to learn a few of these folktales, in Kouri-Vini of course. See **More Resources** (p. 166) to find out where to read them.

# Lesson 18

## *Holidays*

# VOCABULARY

| | |
|---|---|
| Mardi Gra | *Mardi Gras* |
| Karnaval | *Carnival* |
| Vendrédi Sin | *Good Friday* |
| Sammdi Sin | *Holy Saturday* |
| Pak | *Easter* |
| Nwèl, Krismis | *Christmas* |
| Tou-Sin | *All-Saints* |
| Kapitènn | *Capitain* |
| shar | *car; parade float* |
| garoshé, garòsh | *to throw* |
| biy | *bead* |
| Mærkrédi dê Senn | *Ash Wednesday* |
| Nouvel An | *New Year* |
| Bonn Anné! | *Happy New Year!* |
| Révéyon | *Réveillon (New Year's Eve dinner with midnight champagne toast)* |
| fèt | *birthday, party, holiday* |
| fé fèt | *to have a party* |
| gin in bon tem | *to have a good time* |

# DIALOGUE 1

A: Jòrdi çé Karnaval!
B: Wé! N'a gin in bon tem pou Mardi Gra-la!
A: Démin çé Mærkrédi dê Senn é Karèm-la komens.
B: La, no va fé mèg jiska Jour Pak-la.

*A: Today is Carnival!*
*B: Yes! We're going to have a good time for Mardi Gras!*
*A: Tomorrow is Ash Wednesday and Lent begins.*
*B: Then, we're going to fast until Easter Day.*

# DIALOGUE 2

C: Misyé, misyé!
Garòsh mò dê biy!
D: Li pe pa tendé twa.
C: Misyé! Mo la!
D: Li tro lwin astœr.
C: Fé tensyon, mô frær!
D: Mé ki çé li garoshé apré twa?
C: Çé dê biy en vær!
D: Mé m'olé ça osit!

*C: Mister, mister!*
*Throw me some beads!*
*D: He can't hear you.*
*C: Mister! Here I am!*
*D: He's too far away now.*
*C: Look out, brother!*
*D: But what did he throw you?*
*C: It's some glass beads!*
*D: But I want some too!*

**★ LAGNIAPPE ★**

*Éyou nouzòt gin pou kouri astœr?* Where do we go from here? Now it's up to us to use and practice what we've learned! Try meeting up regularly for a with a few friends to keep your Creole sharp; start your own *Latab Kréyòl.* Maybe you have other family members who'd be interested in learning a few phrases of the language too. Don't be afraid to share what you know, and always remember the resources available to you online and elsewhere (listed at the back). *Prenn kouraj é kontiné parlé* — take courage and keep speaking!

# Grammar Sketch

*Nouns: People, Places & Things*

# INTRO TO NOUNS

Nouns are really useful words we can use to name things. First, we'll see how to talk one thing (singular: *shyin* / dog) and more than one thing (plural: *shyin-yé* / the dogs). Also, we'll see how we can talk about something specific ('the dog'), and something non-specific ('a dog').

Some languages classify nouns by gender. Nouns in Creole are like those in English, in the sense that they are are not typically classified by gender. For some speakers of Creole, though, nouns can be masculine or feminine. In this book, we've decided not to include these forms. It introduces a lot of complications which are not necessary for beginning learners that this book is hoping to help, since you will still be speaking great Creole without including these features. Also, not all speakers of Creole do classify nouns by gender. It's good to be aware of it, though, since you may hear it when listening to other speakers of Creole.

### A NOTE ON VARIATION

Here, as with everywhere in this book, you will see that there are a great deal of different ways of expressing the same sort of thing. For example, the word 'languages' might be translated as *langaj*, *langaj-ye* or *lê langaj*. This variation is completely normal: language is dynamic and diverse. Creole is a particularly beautiful example of this diversity. To do justice to the richness of the Creole language, we have attempted to include as many different forms as possible. All of these are equally valid, and you should not worry about any one being 'more correct' than any other. In choosing which forms to use, we suggest you practice your Creole as much as possible with people in your family, your community or even online to a find a way of speaking which feels authentic.

# SINGULAR

Say we just want to talk about some dog, not a particular dog, just 'a dog'. We say 'a' in Creole by using the word ***in***:

> ***in*** *shyin*
> a dog

Some people say ***un***, so you can write it this way too. Also, if ***in*** comes before a vowel, it changes to ***ènn***:

> ***ènn*** *œr*
> an hour

There's another way to mark a noun as non-specific, using nothing at all:

> ***shyin***
> a dog

If you want to talk about a specific thing, 'the dog', mark it with *-la*.

> ***shyin-la***
> the dog

Some people also use *le, la* before the noun.

> *Yé gin* **le drwat** *parlé.*
> They have the right to speak.

> ***La fenm*** *apé péshé.*
> The woman is fishing.

# PLURAL

What about a bunch of dogs? In English, we add -s:
**one dog, two dogs.**

### ★ PLAIN NOUN ★

In Creole, we can just use the noun on its own:

> ***shyin***
> dogs

Context will tell us whether we're talking about one or more of something:

> *No gin **poul**, é no linm yê **dézèf**.*
> We have **chickens**, and we like their **eggs**.

### ★ NOUN + *-YÉ* ★

If we want to specify that a noun is plural, we can add *-yé* to the end:

> *Tou makak trouv sô **piti-yé** joli.*
> Every monkey thinks her **children** are pretty. (proverb)

We can use *-yé* when we want to mark a specific plural noun:

> *Çété tô frèr ki volé **poul-yé**? Non, çé té **vwazin-yé**.*
> Did your brother steal **the chickens**?
> No, it was **the neighbors**.

Ina dé dézèf
dan dézèr

Another way to mark a specific plural noun is by combining the specificity marker *-la* (see above, p. 91) and the plural marker *-yé* to form *-layé*.

> *To volé* ***poul-layé****? Non, çé té* ***vwazin-layé****.*
> Did your brother steal **the chickens**?
> No, it was **the neighbors**.

## ★ LÊ + NOUN ★

Another way to make a noun plural is to add *lê* just before it. If you use this, you can't use *-yé* in addition.

> *Kan to manj krébis, to sis* ***lê tèt****.*
> When I'm eating crawfish, I suck **the heads**.

## ★ DÊ + NOUN ★

If we want to talk about 'some of' something, we can use the word *dê*:

> *Mo mèt* ***dê tomat*** *dan mô gombo.*
> I put **some tomatoes** in my gumbo.

## ★ COUNTING ★

Finally, if we're counting something, we can just add the number — there's no need to use *-yé* or *lê* here.

> *No gin* ***sink poul, trò koshon*** *épi* ***ènn vyé korish.***
> We have **five chickens**, **three pigs** and **one old rooster**.

# PRONOUNS

*Mwa, mo-minm é mo... é mô shyin*
Me, myself and I... and my dog

Pronouns are words we use to talk about things without having to mention the noun over and over again.

### ★ SUBJECT: *MO...* / I... ★

The subject is the one doing the action, the 'I' in 'I eat rice'.

***Li*** *gonn!* ***Mo*** *pa konné éyou* ***li*** *yê.*
**She**'s gone! **I** don't know where **she** is.

***Y'****apé vini astœr.*
**They**'re coming now.

***No*** *linm dansé, mé* ***zòt*** *linm pa ça.*
**We** like to dance, **y'all** don't like that.

| SINGULAR | | PLURAL | |
|---|---|---|---|
| *mo* | I | *nouzòt, no* | we |
| *to*<br>*vou* | you<br>you (formal) | *vouzòt, zòt* | y'all |
| *li* | he, she, it | *yé, ça* | they |

### ★ OBJECT: ...MÒ / ...MWA / ...ME ★

The object is the one the action is done to, the 'me' in 'They like me'.

*Li donn* ***mò*** *ça.*
He gave it to **me**.

*Manj* ***li****!*
Eat **it**!

*Ça va di* ***twa*** *to fou.*
They'll tell **you** you're crazy.

Another use for this form is to emphasize the subject of the sentence by adding it at the beginning or end. You'll probably recognize the distinctive Louisiana flavor of these sentences in English, too:

***Mwa****, mo linm ça!*
**Me**, I like that!

*To kanay,* ***twa****!*
You're mischievous, **you**!

*Li parl kréyòl byin,* ***li****.*
She speaks Creole well, **her**.

| SINGULAR | | PLURAL | |
|---|---|---|---|
| *mwa, mò* | me | *nouzòt, no* | we |
| *twa, tò*<br>*vou* | you<br>you (formal) | *vouzòt, zòt* | y'all |
| *li* | he, she, it | *yé* | they |

### ★ POSSESSIVE: *MÔ* / MY ★

Possessive pronouns show who something belongs to. When we write these pronouns, we use the circumflex (the little hat, ˆ).

> ***mô*** *liv*
> **my** book
>
> ***tô*** *lavi*
> **your** life
>
> ***yê*** *pirog*
> **their** pirogue

Sometimes, you will also come across people using forms like *mê, tê, sê* (for plural nouns) and *mâ, tâ, sâ* (for feminine nouns). Whether or not you use these, your Creole will still sound just fine – and we note them here just to make you aware they exist.

| SINGULAR | | PLURAL | |
|---|---|---|---|
| *mô* | my | *nô* | our |
| *tô*<br>*vô* | your<br>your (formal) | *zô, zòt* | y'all's |
| *sô* | his, hers, its | *yê* | their |

*mo-minm*

**★ REFLEXIVE: *MO-MINM* / MYSELF ★**

If the subject and the object of a verb are the same, we need to use what's called a reflexive pronoun. This is like English 'herself', 'myself', etc.

> *Li parl a* ***li-minm****.*
> She talks to **herself**.
>
> *Mo lav* ***mo-minm*** *apré travay.*
> I wash **myself** after work.

| SINGULAR | | PLURAL | |
|---|---|---|---|
| *mo-minm* | myself | *nou-minm* | ourselves |
| *twa-minm*<br>*vou-minm* | yourself<br>yourself (formal) | *vou-minm, zòt-minm* | yourselves |
| *li-minm* | him, her, itself | *yé-minm* | themselves |

### ★ EMPHATIC POSSESSIVE: *MÔ-CHIN, -KIN, -CHÈNN, -KÈNN* / MY OWN, MINE ★

Emphatic possessive pronouns emphasize whose thing we're talking about, and are equivalent to saying something is 'your *own*' in English. You do this by adding -chin, -kin, -chènn or -kènn to the normal possessive pronoun.

> *M'apé parlé pou* ***mô-chènn*** *mézon.*
> I'm talking about **my own** house.
>
> *Non,* ***nô-chin*** *gombo çé myé.*
> No, **our** gumbo is better!
>
> *Ranj* ***tô-kènn*** *zafœr-yé!*
> Put **your own** stuff away!

They can also stand alone, like 'hers', 'yours' and 'mine' in English:

> *Çé* ***sô-chènn****.*
> It's **hers**.
>
> ***Tô-kin*** *çé pli gran ke* ***mô-kin****.*
> **Yours** is bigger than **mine**.
>
> *Nô famiy çé gran,* ***zô-chènn*** *çé piti.*
> Our family is big, **y'all**'s is small.

| SINGULAR | | PLURAL | |
|---|---|---|---|
| *mô-chin* | my own | *nô-chin* | our own |
| *tô-chin*<br>*vô-chin* | your own<br>your own (formal) | *zô(t)-chin* | y'all's own |
| *sô-chin* | his, her, its own | *yê-chin* | they |

# Grammar Sketch

*Adjectives: Describing things*

Adjectives describe nouns. In English, they usually come before a noun: 'a big house'. In Creole, some adjectives come before the noun, but most come after the noun.

There are a set group of adjectives that come before noun, just like English: *in gran lamézon* / a big house. Some of these adjectives are shown below. Remember this group of adjectives with the mnemonic: adjectives describing **BANGS** — beauty, age, newness, goodness, size — come before the noun.

***bèl*** *zwazo*
**beautiful** bird

***joli*** *shanson*
**pretty** song

***vyé*** *boug*
**old** guy

***nouvo*** *char*
**new** car

***vayan*** *padna*
**good** buddy

***bon*** *tem*
**good** time

***gran*** *lamézon*
**big** house

***ti*** *piti*
**little** child

Apart from the **BANGS** adjectives, the other adjectives all come after the noun they describe.

*shyin* ***las***
**tired** dog

*lamin* ***gosh***
**left** hand

*garçon* ***gayar***
**healthy** boy

*shawi* ***kanay***
**mischievous** raccoon

*moun* ***kréyòl***
**Creole** people

For how to form sentences like 'I'm hungry' or 'My truck is red', see p. 117.

# COMPARATIVES

If you want to compare something to something else, you need to use *pli ... ke* to mean 'more ... than'. Sometimes you can also hear *pli ... pasé* for 'more ... than', and *mwins ... ke* for 'less than'. If you want to say something is equal to something else, you can say *osi ... ke* for 'as ... as'.

*Mo **pli** vyé **ke** twa.*
I'm old**er than** you.

*Tô shawi **pli** kanay **ke** mô-kin.*
Your raccoon is **more** mischievous **than** mine.

*Mô fiy **pli** gran **ke** tô fiy.*
My daughter is tall**er than** your daughter.

*Bouki **pli** vit **pasé** Lapin.*
Bouki is fast**er than** Lapin.

*To **mwins** smat **ke** mwa.*
You're **less** smart **than** me.

*Non, mo **osi** smat **ke** twa!*
No, I'm **as** smart **as** you!

# Grammar Sketch

*Verbs:*
*Doing*
*& Being*

# INTRO TO VERBS

Verbs are among the most important words to learn in a new language. In Louisiana Creole, verbs are not conjugated like they are in French. However, some verbs have more than one form that you will need to learn as well as which forms to use in what situations. First, let's introduce the two main classes of verbs in Louisiana Creole: one-stem verbs and two-stem verbs.

**ONE-STEM VERBS**, as the name suggests, have one invariable form — they never change. An example of a one-stem verb is *bwa*/to drink. Here are some sentences using *bwa*:

> *Li **bwa** in tas kafé shak matin.*
> He **drinks** a cup of coffee every morning.
>
> *Yé té pe pa galopé akoz yé té **bwa** tro.*
> They couldn't run because they'd **drunk** too much.
>
> *Mo p'alé **bwa** dilé-çala.*
> I'm not going to **drink** that milk.

As you can see, even though the three example sentences are all in different tenses (present, past, and future, respectively), the form of the verb bwa does not change.

**TWO-STEM VERBS**, on the other hand, have two forms: a long form and a short form. Which form you use depends on the situation. A common two-stem verb is *parlé, parl,* 'to speak.' Whenever a two-stem verb is listed in this booklet, the long form will be listed first (*parlé*), followed by a comma and the short form (*parl*). Here are some sentences using *parlé, parl*:

> *Fenm-çala **parl** kréyòl.*
> That woman **speaks** Creole.
>
> *Kan li té malad li té pe pa **parlé**.*
> When he was sick, he couldn't **talk**.
>
> *N'a **parlé** talœr.*
> We'll **talk** soon.

In the first example sentence, the short form *parl* is used. In the other two examples, the long form *parlé* is used. It must be noted that not every speaker agrees on which verbs are one-stem and which verbs are two-stem. For example, some speakers translate the verb 'to work' as a two-stem verb: *travayé, travay*. Other speakers translate this verb as a one-stem verb: *travay*. These differences are fairly easy to detect with a bit of practice. But let's return to two-stem verbs. We will be discussing when to use each of these forms — the long one and the short one — in the following sections.

# PRE-VERBAL MARKERS

As we already noted, verbs in Louisiana Creole are not conjugated like in French. Instead of conjugations, Louisiana Creole uses special words placed in front of the verb to indicate things like verb tense. In this way it is similar to the way the future is formed in English:

> I walk (present)
> I will walk (future)

In this instance, the future is indicated by the addition of the pre-verbal marker 'will' in front of the main verb 'walk.' Louisiana Creole uses pre-verbal markers to talk about the future, the conditional, the present progressive, the past progressive, and the anterior past. We will explain each of these forms in turn.

# FUTURE

To form the future tense, we simply add a form of the verb 'to go' in front of the main verb of the sentence. This is similar to English sentences like 'I'm going to learn Spanish.' There are two verbs for 'to go' in Louisiana Creole: *alé/va* and *kouri*. In addition, there is a variant of *va* that only occurs when expressing the future tense: *a*. The most common way to mark the future is to use either *va* or *a*, but some speakers will use the form *alé* in front of the main verb as well. Whatever form of the future marker you use, it is always followed by the long form of the main verb (if it's a two-stem verb). Let's look at a few examples of *va/a*:

> *M'**a** wa mô sœr aswa.*
> **I'll** see my sister tonight.
>
> *To **va** fé ça démin?*
> **Will** you do that tomorrow?
>
> *Vouzòt **va** gin asé tem.*
> Y'all **will** have enough time.

And let's look at a few examples using other forms to express the future:

> *Mo p'**alé** gété TV jòrdi.*
> I'm not **going to** watch TV today.
>
> *Yé **kouri** jwé èk piti-yé.*
> They're **going to** play with the kids.

When you want to say something 'will be' in the future, you use the special word *sa* by itself:

> *Mo **sa** la talœr.*
> **I'll be** there soon.
>
> *Yé **sa** konten.*
> They**'ll be** happy.

# CONDITIONAL

To express the conditional tense in Louisiana Creole, we use the pre-verbal marker *sé*. As was the case with the future tense, the main verb following the marker will be in the long form if it is a two-stem verb. Here are some examples:

*Mo* ***sé*** *kouri èk twa si mo té gin asé tem.*
I **would** go with you if I had enough time.

*Li* ***sé*** *kapab fé ça.*
She **should** be able to do it.

*No* ***sé*** *linmé trò gro zònyon rouj.*
We**'d** like three large red onions.

# PRESENT PROGRESSIVE

To express an ongoing action, we use the pre-verbal marker *apé* or its shortened form, *ap*. This corresponds to English sentences like 'I'm eating an apple right now.' If the main verb is a two-stem verb, we use the long form following *apé/ ap*. Note that the pronouns frequently combine with this pre-verbal marker, so mo *apé* would become *m'apé*. Here are some example sentences:

*L'****apé*** *lir in liv.*
He**'s** read**ing** a book.

*Y'****ap*** *gété syèl-la pou wa soléy-koushé-la.*
They**'re** watch**ing** the sky to see the sunset.

*N'****apé*** *parlé tro fòr.*
We**'re** talk**ing** too loudly.

# PAST PROGRESSIVE

To express an action that was going on in the past, we use two pre-verbal markers. The second one is the same as in the present progressive, *apé/ap*. Before that word we add the marker *té*, but because the work after it starts in a vowel, the two words usually combine to become *t'apé* or *t'ap*. Here are some examples:

*Popa **t'apé** travayé dan lakour kan mo vini.*
Dad **was** work**ing** in the yard when I came.

*Mo **t'ap** dòrmi tandi to t'ap kwi soupé.*
I **was** sleep**ing** while you were cooking supper.

*No **t'apé** marshé bòr lamær.*
We **were** walk**ing** by the sea.

As with the other tenses we have looked at so far, we use the long form of two-stem verbs in the past progressive.

# PAST ANTERIOR

The past anterior is used to talk about actions that were completed in the past prior to another past action. The pre-verbal marker used for the past anterior is *té*. As with other pre-verbal markers, *té* is followed by the long form of two-stem verbs. Here are some examples:

*Li **té** manjé avan li parti.*
He **had** eaten before he left.

*Yé **té** pa ranjé yê shanm.*
They **had**n't cleaned their room.

*To **té** parlé èk li avan to vini isit?*
**Did** you talk to her before coming here?

# SIMPLE PAST

To talk about an action in the simple past, you use the long form of two-stem verbs without any pre-verbal markers. So for instance, let's compare the present and the simple past of the verb *parlé-parl*:

*Nouzòt* ***parl*** *françé.*
We **speak** French.

*Nouzòt* ***parlé*** *françé.*
We **spoke** French.

For one-stem verbs, you simply use the pronoun and the verb. This means that for one-stem verbs, a sentence in the present can look identical to a sentence in the simple past:

*Mo* ***bwa****.*
I **drink**.

*Mo* ***bwa****.*
I **drank**.

So how can we tell the difference? Context will usually make it clear. This is always the case with verbs that denote an action.

Stative verbs — verbs that indicate a state of being — function a little differently. For these verbs, such as *olé*/to want, *kapab*/ to be able, *bezwin*/to need, *gin*/to have, etc., you always need to use *té*, even if it is in the simple past. Here are a few examples:

*Mo* ***té gin*** *kat shar.*
I **had** four cars.

*No* ***té pa kapab*** *vini.*
We **couldn't** come.

*Vou* ***té bezwin*** *in ta larjen.*
Y'all **needed** a lot of money.

## AUXILIARY VERBS

In addition to the pre-verbal markers that we have discussed, there are other verbs that can precede the main verb in a sentence. We have already seen some of them: *olé*/to want, *bezwin*/to need, etc. Just like with pre-verbal markers, auxiliary verbs require us to use the long form of two-stem verbs:

> *Mo* ***bezwin*** *kouri lagrosri.*
> I **need** to go to the grocery store.
>
> *T'****olé*** *diné avèk mò aswa?*
> Do you **want** to have dinner with me tonight?

There are also phrases that function like auxiliary verbs such as *gin pou*/to have to. Here is an example of how it is used:

> *To* ***gin pou*** *kouri shé twa.*
> You **have to** go home.

# 'TO BE'

The verb 'to be' in Louisiana Creole is a bit irregular. In general, the language does not use 'to be' as often as we do in English. In sentences with a noun and an adjective, you do not need to use a form of 'to be.' Examples:

*Li sho.*
It's hot.

*Shyin-çala vilin.*
That dog is mean.

*Mo fim.*
I'm hungry.

However, there are instances where you do need a form of 'to be.' If you are equating two nouns, it's necessary to use *çé*. This form is also used when there is no other explicit subject:

***Çé*** *sho.*
[It]**'s** hot.

*Mo* ***çé*** *mèt-lékol.*
I **am** a teacher.

*Ça* ***çé*** *domaj.*
That**'s** a shame.

When there is no explicit subject and you want to express an idea in the past, you need to combine *çé* with the anterior past marker, *té*. If you are equating two nouns in the past, you only need the marker *té*:

*Çé* ***té*** *sho.*
[It] **was** hot.

*Mo* ***té*** *mèt-lékol.*
I **was** a teacher.

It is also possible to form emphatic sentences with *çé* in instances where it is not necessarily required:

*Li* ***çé*** *sho!*
It**'s** hot!

Another form of the verb 'to be' is *yê*. This form is used in questions and in relative clauses. Here are a few examples:

*Éyou to* ***yê****?*
Where **are** you?

*Mo konten konm mo* ***yê****.*
I'm happy the way I **am**.

*Ki moun nonm-la* ***yê****?*
Who **is** that man?

A third form of the verb 'to be' is *dèt*. This form corresponds to the infinitive. It is used in commands and when it follows auxiliary verbs or pre-verbal markers. Here are some examples:

***Dèt pa*** *tar!*
**Don't be** late!

*To sé linmé* ***dèt*** *bòs-la?*
Would you like **to be** the boss?

*Li olé* ***dèt*** *in doktœr ékan li vini gran.*
She wants **to be** a doctor when she grows up.

Finally, to use the verb 'to be' in the future, you can either combine *va* (future marker) and *dèt* (infinitive) or use the marker *sa* introduced under the section about the future tense:

*No* ***va dèt*** *tar.*
We **will be** late.

*No* ***sa*** *tar.*
We **will be** late.

## IMPERATIVES

In order to express commands in Louisiana Creole, we generally use to short form of two-stem verbs; obviously one-stem verbs use their invariant form. There are some speakers who make a distinction between formal and informal commands. For these speakers, the short form of a two-stem verb is informal and the long stem is formal. Here are some examples:

> ***Donn*** *mò kishòj pou manjé.*
> **Give** me something to eat.
>
> ***Parl*** *kréyòl ékan to parl èk mò.*
> **Speak** Creole when you talk to me.
>
> ***Travay*** *smat, pa dur.*
> **Work** smart, not hard.

# NEGATION

In addition to affirmative/positive statements, it is important to know how to make negative statements. The most common negative particle in Louisiana Creole is *pa*. Its position in a sentence depends partially on the tense of the sentence. If the sentence is in the present, *pa* will come after the verb:

*Li manj* ***pa*** *lavyònn.*
He **doesn't** eat meat.

*Yé parl* ***pa*** *mérikin.*
They **don't** speak English.

*No travay* ***pa*** *la.*
We **don't** work there.

In the simple past, pa comes before the verb. Remember to use the long stem if it is a two-stem verb:

*Li* ***pa*** *manjé lavyònn.*
He **didn't** eat meat.

*Yé* ***pa*** *parlé mérikin.*
They **didn't** speak English.

*No* ***pa*** *travayé la.*
We **didn't** work there.

It is also important to note that certain verbs (principally auxiliary verbs and stative verbs) always come after *pa*, even if they are in the present tense. These verbs are very frequent in the language, and it will only take a little practice to recognize which ones behave this way. Here are a few examples:

*No* ***pa konné****.*
We **don't know**.

*Zòt* ***pa gin*** *asé.*
Y'all **don't have** enough.

*Yé* ***p'olé*** *ça*
They **don't want** that.

*Li* ***pa bezwin*** *tou ça.*
He **doesn't need** all that.

When there are pre-verbal markers in the sentence such as *té*, *sé*, or *va/a*, *pa* comes after the marker. The one exception, however, is *apé/ap*:

> *L'apé marshé dousmen.*
> She is walking slowly.
>
> *Li **p'**ap marshé dousmen.*
> She is**n't** walking slowly.

Other phrases you might encounter in negative sentences include *pa aryin*/nothing, *pa pærsonn*/no one, *pa nil-plas*/ nowhere, etc. In these phrases, the placement of *pa* corresponds to the rules we mentioned above. The other part of the phrase follows the verb unless the sentence is in the present tense, in which case it follows *pa*. Here are a few examples:

> *Li **pa** wa **pærsonn**.*
> He **didn't** see **anyone**. (He saw no one.)
>
> *To manj **pa aryin**.*
> You **don't** eat **anything**. (You eat nothing.)
>
> *Mo té **pa** kouri **nil-plas**.*
> I **didn't** go **anywhere**. (I went nowhere.)

One common negative word that does not require the use of *pa*, however, is *jamé*/never. It generally gets placed wherever *pa* would be placed. If the two words co-occur, *jamé* follows *pa*:

> *Mo (**pa**) **jamé** wa li.*
> I **never** saw it.

Multiple negative words/phrases can be combined within the same sentence:

> *Mo pa jamin wa pærsonn apé kouri nil-plas.*
> I never saw anyone going anywhere.

# ADVERBS

Adverbs describe how an action is done. These words generally follow the main verb, but there is some flexibility concerning where an adverb appears in a sentence. Common adverbs and adverbial phrases involve time and place. Here are a few examples of adverbs and adverbial phrases in Louisiana Creole:

*Nouzòt parl kréyol **touléjour**.*
We speak Creole **everyday**.

*Zenfan-yé apé jwé **déyòr**.*
The children are playing **outside**.

*Yé t'apé rodayé **obòr isit**.*
They were wandering **around here**.

Adverbs can also modify adjectives. In these instances, the adverb precedes whatever adjective it is modifying:

*Fenm-la té **jolimen** bèl.*
The woman was **very** beautiful.

*Li **byin** kanay, la.*
He's **real** sly, that one.

*No **mòyær** las astær.*
We're **kind of** tired now.

# Grammar Sketch

*Sentences:*

*Putting it all together*

# WORD ORDER

In Louisiana Creole, like English, there is a set order of words in a sentence: subject-verb-object. Remember that pronouns (p. 95) take different forms depending on whether they are subject or object, like 'I' and 'me' in English.

> *Mo linm twa.*
> I love you.
>
> *To linm mwa.*
> You love me.

In this section, we'll look at some more complex kinds of sentences so you can put together everything you've learned so far.

# YES-NO QUESTIONS

There are a couple of different ways of turning a statement into a question. Just like English, you can raise your intonation at the end of a sentence, keeping the structure the same:

> *T'olé manjé.*
> You want to eat.
>
> *T'olé manjé?*
> You want to eat?

You can also use the question word *èske* at the start of the question. This is like 'Do you...?' in English.

> ***Èske*** *t'olé manjé?*
> **Do** you want to eat?

# WH-QUESTIONS

If you're asking **who, what, when, where, why** or **how**, the structure you use is similar to yes-no questions, but you have to add those wh-words.

### * WHO *

***Ki moun*** *li yê?*
**Who** is he?

***Ça ki*** *konné?*
**Who** knows?

***Ki*** *Jeff yê?*
**Who** is Jeff?

### * WHAT *

***Ki kalité*** *tròk to gin?*
**What kind** of truck do you have?

***Ki lè*** *t'olé jwènn?*
**What time** do you want to meet?

***Ça ki*** *sô non?*
**What**'s his name?

***Ki*** *çé ça?*
**What** is that?

***Ça*** *t'olé?*
**What** do you want?

***Ça*** *t'apé parlé pou?*
**What** are you talking about?

## ★ WHEN ★

***Ékan*** *to gonn?*
**When** are you leaving?

***Kan*** *to vyin bæk?*
**When** are you coming back?

## ★ WHERE ★

***Éyou*** *to sòr?*
**Where** are you from?

***Éyou*** *to rès?*
**Where** do you live?

## ★ WHY ★

***Kòfær*** *to tris?*
**Why** are you sad?

## ★ HOW ★

***Komen*** *to yê?*
**How** are you?

***Komen*** *to kwi tô gombo?*
**How** do you cook your gumbo?

If you ask a question with the verb 'to be', remember you need to use *yê* (p. 112).

# RELATIVE CLAUSES

Sometimes, we want to use a whole sentence to describe a noun. This sentence-within-a-sentence is called a relative clause. An example from English is 'The man, who I met yesterday'. Or: 'The man I met yesterday'. Both of these structures are also possible in Creole:

> *Nonm-la mo jwènn yœr.*
> The man I met yesterday.
>
> *Nonm-la,* ***ki*** *mo jwènn yœr.*
> The man, **whom** I met yesterday.

You can also modify a longer phrase with a relative clause and *ki:*

> *Mo gin in kouzin* ***ki*** *travay o Tèksas.*
> I have a cousin **who** works in Texas.

Sometimes, we want to talk about the relative clause itself, as in 'I like **what you're cooking**'. In these cases we can use *ça* or *ça ki.*

> *Li manjé* ***ça ki*** *mo kwi.*
> She ate **what** I cooked for her.
>
> *Fé* ***ça*** *t'olé!*
> Do **what** you want!
>
> *Piti gin pou fé* ***ça*** *yê paren di yé fé.*
> Kids have to do **what** their parents tell them to do.

Other times, we want to talk about where something is. For this, we can use the word *éyou* (you will also hear its variants *aou, ou, ayou,* etc.).

> *Vilaj mo té né é élvé.*
> The town where I was born and raised.
>
> *Bayou* ***éyou*** *no fé lashash.*
> The bayou **where** we go hunting.
>
> *Li té pa kapab trouvé* ***éyou*** *sô shyin té.*
> He couldn't find **where** his dog was.
>
> ***Éyou*** *no rès, li joli.*
> **Where** we live, it's pretty.

# Lexicon

*Creole–English*

## A – a

| | |
|---|---|
| **a** | *aux.* future marker |
| **a** | *prep.* of; to; from; at |
| **abichud** | *aux.* used to |
| **(l)abitan** | *n.* farmer |
| **(l)abri** | *n.* shelter |
| **adrwa** | *adv.* right (direction) |
| **Afrikin; afrikin** | *n, adj.* African |
| **agosh** | *adv.* left |
| **(l)aj** | *n.* age |
| **aklé** | *v.* lock |
| **akoz** | *conj.* because |
| **alentour** | *prep.* approximately; around; about |
| **alé** | *v.* go |
| **alfabèt** | *n.* alphabet |
| **alman** | *n, adj.* German |
| **alon** | *aux.* let's |
| **alòr** | *interj.* then; so; Fr. 'donc' |
| **(z)ami** | *n.* friend |
| **(l)amour** | *n.* love |
| **(l)amourè** | *n.* boyfriend; lover (male) |
| **(z)an** | *n.* year (for counting age) |
| **(l)andoui** | *n.* andouille (sausage) |
| **(l)ané** | *n.* year |
| **anmær** | *adj.* bitter |
| **ap(é)** | *aux.* progressive marker |
| **aprenn** | *v.* learn; teach |
| **apré** | *adv, prep.* after |
| **aprémidi** | *nphr.* afternoon |
| **aout** | *n.* August |
| **arété, arèt** | *v.* stop |
| **arivé, ariv** | *v.* arrive; happen |
| **ariyin** | *n.* nothing |
| **asé** | *adv.* enough |
| **asit** | *v.* sit |
| **astœr** | *adv.* now |
| **aswa** | *n.* tonight |
| **ashté, ashèt** | *v.* buy |

| | |
|---|---|
| **fé atensyon** | *phr.* be careful |
| **avan** | *adv.* before |
| **avansé, avans** | *v.* progress |
| **aværti** | *v.* warn |
| **avèk** | *conj.* with |
| **avril** | *n.* April |

# B – b

| | |
|---|---|
| **babìnn** | *n.* lip |
| **bal** | *n.* dance (social gathering) |
| **balé** | *n.* broom |
| **balé, bal** | *v.* sweep |
| **baloté, balot** | *v.* stagger |
| **(la)bank** | *n.* bank |
| **banndjo** | *n.* banjo |
| **(la)barb** | *n.* beard |
| **barbi** | *n.* catfish |
| **barbouyé, barbouy** | *v.* dirty; get dirty |
| **baré, bar** | *v.* lock; block |
| **bat** | *v.* fight; beat |
| **bati** | *v.* build |
| **batimen** | *n.* ship |
| **batimen-d-ær** | *n.* airplane |
| **batis** | *n.* building |
| **bato** | *n.* boat |
| **baton** | *n.* stick |
| **baton-mayi** | *nphr.* cornstalk |
| **bayou** | *n.* bayou |
| **bæk** | *adj.* back |
| **bezwin** | *v.* need |
| **béñé** | *n.* beignet |
| **bétay** | *n.* livestock |
| **bèf** | *n.* cow |
| **bèl** | *n.* girlfriend; female lover |
| **bèl** | *adj.* beautiful |
| **bèl-fiy** | *n.* daughter-in-law |
| **bèl-mær** | *n.* mother-in-law; stepmother |
| **bèl-sœr** | *n.* sister-in-law |
| **bèñé, bèñ** | *v.* swim; bathe |
| **bèt** | *adj, n.* stupid; animal |
| **(La)Bib** | *n.* Bible |
| **bisik** | *n.* bicycle |
| **biy** | *n.* bead |
| **blan** | *adj.* white |
| **blanshi** | *v.* whitewash |
| **blésé, blès** | *v.* injure |
| **bliyé, bliy** | *v.* forget |
| **bo-fis** | *n.* son-in-law |
| **bo-fræ r** | *n.* brother-in-law |
| **bokou** | *adj, adv.* many; very |
| **bon** | *adj.* good |
| **Bondjè** | *n.* God |
| **bonjou** | *interj.* hello |
| **bon-marshé** | *adj.* cheap |
| **Bonn fèt!** | *phr.* Happy birthday! |
| **bonn-aryin** | *adj.* good-for-nothing |
| **bonnœr** | *adj.* early |
| **bonswa** | *interj.* good evening; good night |
| **bo-pær** | *n.* father-in-law; stepfather |
| **boskoyo** | *n.* cypress knee |
| **bòl** | *n.* bowl |
| **bòs** | *n.* boss |
| **bòt** | *n.* boots |
| **(la)bou** | *n.* mud |
| **boudin** | *n.* boudin (sausage) |
| **boug** | *n.* guy; man |
| **bouklé, bouk** | *v.* buckle |
| **(la)boukònn** | *n.* smoke |
| **boukònné** | *v, adj.* smoke (meat); smoked |
| **boulværsé, boulværs** | *v.* upset; change suddenly |
| **bounda** | *n.* butt |
| **(la)boush** | *n.* mouth |
| **(la)boushri** | *n.* boucherie |
| **bout** | *n.* end (of object) |
| **bout-d-tem** | *nphr.* a while |
| **boutéy** | *n.* bottle |
| **boutik** | *n.* store |
| **bouyi, bouy** | *v.* boil |
| **bra** | *n.* arm |
| **branshaj** | *n.* twigs; kindling |

| | |
|---|---|
| **brenm** | *n.* eggplant |
| **brilé, bril** | *v.* burn |
| **brilmen** | *n.* burn |
| **brilmen-lèstoma** | *nphr.* heartburn |
| **briyé, briy** | *v.* shine |
| **brizé, briz** | *v.* shatter |
| **bwa** | *v.* drink |
| **bwason** | *n.* drink |
| **bwat** | *n.* box |
| **(la)byær** | *n.* beer |
| **byin** | *adj, adv.* good; well; very |

# Ç – ç

| | |
|---|---|
| **ça** | *pro.* that; what; it; they |
| **ça-fé** | *conj.* so |
| **-çala** | *det.* that |
| **-ça(la)yé** | *det.* those |
| **ça...?** | *conj.* what...? |
| **çé** | *v.* be |
| **çé té** | *vphr.* it was |
| **-çila** | *det.* this |
| **-çi(la)yé** | *det.* these |

# CH – ch

| | |
|---|---|
| **chak** | *adj.* drunk |
| **chaké, chak** | *v.* get drunk |
| **chéké, chèk** | *v.* check |
| **chi** | *n.* butt |
| **-chin** | *emphatic possessive* (see Grammar Sketch, p. 99) |
| **(la)chirout** | *n.* diarrhea |
| **chombo** | *v.* hold |
| **choué, chou** | *v.* kill |

# D – d

| | |
|---|---|
| **dakòr** | *interj, n, adj.* agreed |
| **dan** | *prep.* in |
| **dansé, dans** | *v.* dance |
| **dærñær** | *adj.* last |
| **dæryær** | *prep.* behind |
| **demi** | *n.* half (used in telling time) |
| **den** | *n.* tooth |
| **dé** | *n.* two |
| **débout** | *adj, adv.* standing; awake |
| **défi** | *n.* challenge |
| **défwa** | *adv.* sometimes |
| **dégouté** | *adj.* disgusted; depressed |
| **déjœné, déjœn** | *n, v.* breakfast; eat breakfast |
| **dékourajé** | *v, adj.* discouraged; discourage |
| **déménajé, déménaj** | *v.* move house |
| **démin** | *n.* tomorrow |
| **dépi** | *prep.* since |
| **désemb** | *n.* December |
| **désenn** | *v.* go down; get off |
| **dési** | *prep.* on top; over |
| **détèsté, détès** | *v.* dislike |
| **dévan** | *prep.* in front of |
| **fé (sô) dévwa** | *vphr.* do one's homework |
| **déyòr** | *adv, prep.* outdoors; outside; out |
| **dézolé** | *adj.* sorry |
| **dézòrd** | *adj, n.* unruly; wild; disorder |
| **dèt** | *v.* be (imperative); be (infinitive) |
| **dèzyèm** | *adj.* second |
| **di** | *v.* say; tell |
| **dibonm** | *n.* mint |

| | |
|---|---|
| **dibœr** | *n.* butter |
| **dibwa** | *n.* wood; woods |
| **difé** | *n.* fire |
| **diféren** | *adj.* different |
| **diférens** | *n.* difference |
| **difwin** | *n.* hay |
| **digri** | *n.* grits |
| **diji** | *n.* juice |
| **dilé** | *n.* milk |
| **dimansh** | *n.* Sunday |
| **Dimansh Ramo** | *nphr.* Palm Sunday |
| **dimyèl** | *n.* honey |
| **diné, dinn** | *n, v.* lunch; eat lunch |
| **dipin** | *n.* bread |
| **diré, dir** | *v.* last (for a while) |
| **diri** | *n.* rice |
| **dis** | *n.* ten |
| **disan** | *n.* blood |
| **disik** | *n.* sugar |
| **dis-sèt** | *n.* seventeen |
| **dité** | *n.* tea |
| **diven** | *n.* wind |
| **divin** | *n.* wine |
| **diz-nèf** | *n.* nineteen |
| **diz-wit** | *n.* eighteen |
| **do** | *interj.* though (discourse particle) |
| **dolo** | *n.* water |
| **dolo ho** | *nphr.* flood |
| **domaj** | *n.* shame; damage |
| **donn** | *v.* give |
| **dòrmi, dòr** | *v.* sleep |
| **dòt** | *adj.* other |
| **dou** | *adj.* sweet |
| **dousmen** | *adj, adv.* slow; slowly |
| **douz** | *n.* twelve |
| **drèt-la** | *prep.* right here; right then |
| **dri** | *adj.* thick (with); heavy |
| **dròl** | *adj.* funny; weird |
| **drwa** | *adj, n.* right |
| **gin drwa** | *vphr.* allowed to |
| **dur** | *adj.* hard; difficult |
| **dursi** | *v.* harden |
| **dwa** | *n.* finger |
| **dwa** | *v.* have to; must |
| **d(e)** | *prep.* from; of |
| **dê** | *adj.* some |

# DJ – dj

| | |
|---|---|
| **djaz** | *n, adj.* jazz |
| **djèp** | *n.* wasp |
| **djòb** | *n.* job |
| **djòg** | *n.* jug |
| **(la)djœl** | *n.* mouth (informal) |

# E – e

| | |
|---|---|
| **embarasé** | *v, adj.* bother; embarrass |
| **embrasé, embras** | *v.* hug; kiss |
| **en** | *prep.* on; in |
| **enba** | *prep.* below; under |
| **endan** | *prep.* inside |
| **endéyòr** | *prep.* outside; outside of |
| **enfamiy** | *adj.* pregnant |
| **enho** | *prep.* on; above |
| **enkòr** | *adj, adv.* yet |
| **enlær** | *adv, adj.* up; on; above |
| **enmærdé, enmærd** | *v, adj.* annoy |
| **ennaryær** | *prep.* in back; behind |
| **ennavan** | *prep.* in front of |
| **ennwiyé** | *adj.* bored; lonesome |
| **ensenm** | *adj.* together |
| **Envil** | *n.* New Orleans |

# É – é

| | | | |
|---|---|---|---|
| **é** | *conj.* and | **étærné, étærn** | *v.* sneeze |
| **édé, èd** | *v.* help | **étidyan** | *n.* student |
| **ékan** | *adv, conj.* when | **étidyé, étidi** | *v.* study |
| **ékri** | *v.* write | **étòné** | *adj.* surprised |
| **épi** | *conj.* and | **étoufé, étouf** | *v.* stew; smother |
| **épis** | *n.* spice | **éyou** | *conj.* where |
| **étærné** | *n.* airplane | | |

# È – è

| | | | |
|---|---|---|---|
| **ègzamp** | *n.* example | **ènn-a-lòt** | *n.* each other |
| **èksplozé** | *v.* explode | **èske** | *conj.* do you...? |
| **èl** | *pro.* she; her | **èskizé, èskiz** | *v.* excuse |
| **èlvé, (è)lèv** | *v.* raise; grow | **èspær (pou)** | *v.* wait (for) |
| **èndjòy** | *v.* enjoy | | |

# F – f

| | | | |
|---|---|---|---|
| **famiy** | *n.* family | **fimé, fimm** | *v.* smoke tobacco |
| **faroush** | *adj.* wild; untamed | **fimyé** | *n.* manure |
| **fé fars** | *vphr.* joke | **fin** | *n.* end |
| **fær-a-shwal** | *n.* horseshoe | **(la)finèt** | *n.* window |
| **færmé, færm** | *v.* close; shut | **fini** | *v.* finish; complete |
| **fenm** | *n.* woman; wife | **fin-lasmèn** | *n.* weekend |
| **fé** | *v.* do; make | **fiy** | *n.* girl; daughter |
| **févi** | *n.* okra | **fiyèl** | *n.* goddaughter |
| **féy** | *n.* leaf | **fiyo** | *n.* godson |
| **fèb** | *adj.* weak | **flèri** | *v.* bloom |
| **(la)fèt** | *n.* birthday; party; holiday | **flœr** | *n.* flower |
| **fèvriyé** | *n.* February | **fo** | *adj.* false |
| **fid** | *n.* animal feed | **fon** | *adj, n.* deep; depths |
| **(la)figur** | *n.* face | **fonn** | *n.* fun |
| **fil** | *n.* wire; string | **fonn** | *n.* phone |
| **fil-a-kroshé** | *n.* barbed wire | **fonsé** | *adj.* dark (of color) |
| **filé** | *n.* filé | **foré** | *n.* forest |
| **fim** | *adj.* hungry | **(la)fot** | *n.* fault |

| | |
|---|---|
| **fò** | *n.* pho (Vietnamese soup) |
| **fònné, fònn** | *v.* wilt |
| **fòr** | *adj.* strong; loud |
| **fou** | *n.* oven |
| **fou** | *adj.* crazy |
| **fou pa mal** | *vphr.* not care; not give a flyin' fiddlestick |
| **foursh** | *n.* pitchfork |
| **fourshèt** | *n.* fork (for eating) |
| **foutimen** | *adv.* extremely |
| **Françé; françé** | *n.* French |
| **fræ̀r** | *n.* brother |
| **frédi** | *v.* get cold |
| **(la)frèsh** | *n.* breeze; shade; relief |
| **frèsh** | *adj.* fresh; cool |
| **frèt** | *adj.* cold |
| **fri** | *v.* fry |
| **frikasé, frikas** | *n, v.* fricassee; stew; stew |
| **fromaj** | *n.* cheese |
| **frwi** | *n.* fruit |
| **fwa** | *n.* time |
| **fyansé** | *v, adj.* engaged |
| **fyær** | *adj.* proud |

# G – g

| | |
|---|---|
| **galimacha** | *n.* jumble; mess |
| **galopé laboush** | *vphr.* chatter; run one's mouth |
| **galopé, galòp** | *v.* run; manage |
| **(la)galri** | *n.* porch |
| **ganñé, ganñ** | *v.* win; earn |
| **garaj** | *n.* garage |
| **garçon** | *n.* boy; son |
| **gardé, gar** | *v.* look at; seem like; watch |
| **gar-manjé** | *n.* pantry |
| **garoshé, garòsh** | *v.* throw |
| **gato** | *n.* cake (general) |
| **gayar** | *adj.* healthy |
| **gazolinn** | *n.* gasoline |
| **gém** | *n.* game |
| **géri** | *v.* heal; cure |
| **gérison** | *n.* cure |
| **gété, gèt** | *v.* watch; look at |
| **gin** | *v.* have |
| **gin pou** | *vphr.* have to |
| **gita** | *n.* guitar |
| **(la)glas** | *n.* ice; ice cream; frost |
| **glasyær** | *n.* refrigerator |
| **(la)gli** | *n.* slime |
| **gogo** | *n.* butt |
| **gombo** | *n.* gumbo |
| **gonn** | *v, adj.* leave; gone |
| **gosh** | *adj.* left (as opposed to right); awkward; clumsy |
| **Gòlf** | *n.* Gulf of Mexico |
| **gout** | *n.* drop |
| **gouté, gou** | *v.* taste |
| **gran** | *adj.* big; tall |
| **grandi** | *v.* grow up; grow |
| **gran-mær/gran-moman** | *n.* grandmother/grandma |
| **gran-moun** | *n.* grow-up |
| **gran-paren** | *n.* grandparents |
| **gran-pær/gran-popa** | *n.* grandfather/grandpa |
| **gran-ouvær** | *adjphr.* wide open |
| **gran-ti-zenfan** | *n.* great-grandchild |
| **graté, grat** | *v.* scratch |
| **grènn** | *n.* seed |
| **gril** | *n.* grill |
| **griyé, griy** | *v.* grill; roast |
| **gro** | *adj.* big; fat |
| **gro tem/mové tem** | *n.* bad weather; storm |
| **grosi** | *v.* grow; grow up; get fat |
| **(la)grosri** | *n.* grocery store |
| **fé grosri** | *vphr.* go grocery shopping |
| **grouyé, grouy** | *v.* move; shake |

# H – h

| | |
|---|---|
| **(la)hansh** | *n.* hip |
| **(la)hash** | *n.* axe |
| **hé!** | *interj.* hey! |
| **hélé, hèl** | *v.* yell; shout |
| **hont** | *n.* shame |
| **hòl** | *n.* dancehall |

# I – i

| | |
|---|---|
| **ibou** | *n.* owl |
| **ifo** | *phr.* need to (do something) |
| **imid** | *adj.* humid |
| **impòrtan** | *adj.* important |
| **impòsib** | *adj.* impossible |
| **in** | *n.* one; a(n) |
| **in lòt/in nòt** | *prep.* another |
| **in pe** | *n.* a little |
| **in ta** | *nphr.* a lot |
| **ina** | *vphr.* there is/are |
| **inavé** | *vphr.* there was/were |
| **inik** | *adj.* unique |
| **Insiswatil** | *phr.* Amen |
| **intérèsé** | *adj.* interesting; interested |
| **isit** | *prep.* here |
| **italyin** | *adj., n.* Italian |
| **itil** | *adj.* useful |
| **itou** | *conj.* also; too |
| **izé** | *adj.* easy |
| **izé, iz** | *v.* use |

# J – j

| | |
|---|---|
| **jakèt** | *n.* jacket |
| **jamb** | *n.* leg |
| **jambalaya** | *n.* jambalaya |
| **jamé** | *adv.* never; ever |
| **janvyé** | *n.* January |
| **japé, jap** | *v.* bark |
| **jardin** | *n.* garden |
| **jardinaj** | *n.* vegetables |
| **jédi** | *n.* Thursday |
| **jélé, jèl** | *v.* freeze |
| **jété, jèt** | *v.* throw; get rid of |
| **jilyèt** | *n.* July |
| **jiska** | *prep.* until |
| **(la)jistis** | *n.* justice |
| **jish** | *adv.* just |
| **jnou** | *n.* knee |
| **joli** | *adj.* pretty; beautiful |
| **jolimen** | *adv.* pretty much; essentially; basically |
| **jonglé, jong (pou/enho/apré)** | *v.* think about |
| **jonn** | *adj.* yellow |
| **jozé** | *n.* blouse |
| **jòrdi** | *n.* today |
| **jœn** | *adj.* young |
| **joué, jou** | *v.* play |
| **jour** | *n.* day |
| **(la)journé** | *n.* day; daytime |
| **(la)jwa** | *n.* joy |
| **jwènn** | *v.* meet |
| **jwif** | *n, adj.* Jewish |
| **jwin** | *n.* June |

# K – k

| | |
|---|---|
| **kabinèt** | *n.* closet |
| **kadjin** | *adj., n.* Cajun |
| **Kadjin** | *n.* Cajun person |
| **kado** | *n.* gift |
| **fé kado** | *vphr.* give as a gift |
| **kafé** | *n.* coffee |
| **kagou** | *adj.* out of sorts |
| **kaka** | *v, n.* poop |
| **kalçon** | *n.* underwear |
| **kalin** | *n, adj.* boyfriend; lover (male); lazy |
| **kalinn** | *n.* girlfriend; lover (female) |
| **kalité** | *n.* kind; type; sort |
| **kammòmèl** | *n.* chamomile |
| **(la)kamponñ** | *n.* country; countryside |
| **kan** | *adv, conj.* when |
| **kanar** | *n.* duck |
| **kanay** | *adj.* cunning; mischievious; sly |
| **kanminm** | *conj.* although |
| **(dé)kann** | *n.* sugarcane |
| **kapab** | *aux.* able; can |
| **kapitènn** | *n.* captain |
| **kapo** | *n.* coat |
| **karankro** | *n.* buzzard; vulture; Carencro |
| **karant** | *n.* forty |
| **karant-é-ènn** | *n.* fourty-one |
| **Karèm** | *n.* Lent |
| **Karnaval** | *n.* Mardi Gras |
| **karòt** | *n.* carrot |
| **kart** | *n.* card |
| **kasé, kas** | *v.* break; crack; shuck; shell |
| **kashé** | *v, adj.* hide; hidden |
| **kat** | *n.* four |
| **Katolik** | *n, adj.* Catholic |
| **katòrz** | *n.* fourteen |
| **katré-vin** | *n.* eighty |
| **katré-vin-dis** | *n.* ninety |
| **(la)kav** | *n.* basement; pantry |
| **kawènn** | *n.* snapping turtle |
| **kayé** | *n.* cottage cheese |
| **ke** | *conj.* than; that |

| | |
|---|---|
| **(la)ké** | *n.* tail |
| **kék** | *n.* cake |
| **kèk** | *adj.* some |
| **kèkènn** | *pro.* someone |
| **kèkènn dòt** | *pro.* someone else |
| **kèk plas** | *n.* somewhere |
| **kèk zafær** | *n.* something |
| **kèl** | *conj.* which; what |
| **kèl...?** | *conj.* what...? |
| **kèstyon** | *n.* question |
| **ki** | *conj.* who; what; that (in relative clauses) |
| **ki ça...?** | *conj.* what...? |
| **ki çé...?** | *conj.* what...? |
| **ki moun** | *conjphr.* who |
| **kiki** | *onom.* haha |
| **kilot** | *n.* pants |
| **kilot kout** | *nphr.* shorts |
| **kinz** | *n.* fifteen |
| **kiréy** | *n.* squirrel |
| **kiriyé** | *adj.* curious; nosy |
| **kishòj** | *n.* thing; something |
| **kité, kit** | *v.* leave; let |
| **kiyær** | *n.* spoon |
| **(la)kizinn** | *n.* kitchen |
| **ki...?** | *conj.* what...? |
| **klær** | *adj, adv.* clear; light (said of skin); clearly |
| **klærmen** | *adv.* clearly |
| **(la)klé** | *n.* key |
| **klo** | *n.* field |
| **klo lwil** | *n.* oilfield |
| **klœb** | *n.* club; nightclub |
| **klou** | *n.* nail |
| **klouk** | *n.* male genitalia |
| **klouyé, klou** | *v.* nail |
| **kokiy** | *n.* shell |
| **kokodri** | *n.* alligator |
| **kolær** | *n, adj.* anger; angry |
| **kombyin** | *adv.* how many |
| **komen** | *conj.* how |

| | |
|---|---|
| **komensé, komens** | *v.* start; begin |
| **komod** | *n.* toilet |
| **(la)kompoñi** | *n.* company (people) |
| **komprenn** | *v.* understand |
| **koné** | *v.* know; can; able |
| **koné** | *aux.* do regularly |
| **konm** | *adj.* like |
| **konm-çi-konm-ça** | *adjphr.* so-so |
| **konsèy** | *n.* advice |
| **konten** | *adj.* happy |
| **kontiné** | *v.* continue |
| **konværsasyon** | *n.* conversation |
| **koñé, koñ** | *v.* hit; strike; bump |
| **korish** | *n.* rooster |
| **koshon** | *n.* pig |
| **koté** | *prep.* at; near |
| **koton** | *n.* cotton |
| **kozé, kòz** | *v.* chat |
| **kòfær** | *conj.* why |
| **kòmærs** | *n.* gossip |
| **fé kòmærs** | *vphr.* cause trouble; make a mess |
| **(la)kònésans** | *n.* act of meeting someone |
| **kòp** | *n.* cup |
| **kòrèk** | *adj.* correct; fine |
| **kòrn** | *n.* horn |
| **kòton-mayi** | *n.* corncob |
| **kœr** | *n.* heart |

| | |
|---|---|
| **(la)kour** | *n.* yard |
| **kou** | *n.* neck |
| **koulœr** | *n.* color |
| **koundjay** | *n.* a type of dance |
| **koupé, koup** | *v.* cut |
| **kouri** | *v.* go |
| **koushé, koush** | *v.* go to bed; lie down |
| **koushkoush** | *n.* cornbread with sugar and milk |
| **koushmar** | *n.* nightmare |
| **kout** | *adj.* short |
| **kouté, kout** | *v.* listen; cost |
| **kouto** | *n.* knife |
| **kouvær** | *adj.* cloudy; covered |
| **kouzin** | *n.* cousin (male or female) |
| **kouzinn** | *n.* cousin (female) |
| **krab** | *n.* crab |
| **krapo** | *n.* toad |
| **krashé, krash** | *v.* spit |
| **krébis** | *n.* crawfish |
| **kréyòl** | *adj., n.* Creole (language, culture, etc.) |
| **krévé, krèv** | *v.* die |
| **Kréyòl** | *n.* Creole person |
| **Krismis** | *n.* Christmas |
| **krò** | *v.* believe; think |
| **kwa** | *conj.* what |
| **kwi** | *v.* cook |

# L – l

| | |
|---|---|
| **la** | *prep, conj.* there; here; then |
| **-la** | *det.* the |
| **laba** | *prep.* there; over there |
| **fé lakònésans (avèk)** | *vphr.* meet (someone for the first time) |
| **fé lakour** | *nphr.* court; date |
| **(la)lamp** | *n.* lamp |
| **(la)lanng** | *n.* tongue |
| **lañap** | *n.* lagniappe |

| | |
|---|---|
| **lapé** | *n.* peace |
| **fé (sô) lapriyè** | *vphr.* say (one's) prayers; pray |
| **larjen** | *n.* money |
| **las** | *adj.* tired |
| **gin lashans** | *phr.* lucky |
| **lashans** | *n.* hunting |
| **lashas** | *n.* hunting |
| **lavé, lav** | *v.* wash |
| **Lavil** | *n.* New Orleans |
| **Lavonn** | *n.* Advent |

| | |
|---|---|
| **lay** | *n.* garlic |
| **la, le, lê** | *det.* the |
| **léçon** | *n.* lesson; moral |
| **légliz** | *n.* church |
| **léjé** | *adj.* light; thin |
| **lékòl** | *n.* school |
| **léritaj** | *n.* heritage |
| **lésé, lès** | *v.* leave; let |
| **léta** | *n.* state |
| **Létazini** | *n.* USA |
| **lété** | *n.* summer |
| **létwal** | *n.* star |
| **lévé, lèv** | *v.* get up; raise |
| **lézar** | *n.* lizard |
| **gin lè** | *vphr.* seem; appear |
| **lèd** | *adj.* ugly |
| **lès** | *n, adj.* east; eastern |
| **lèskalyé** | *n.* stairs; staircase |
| **Lèspañol** | *adj, n.* Spanish (language); Spaniard |
| **lèspri** | *n.* spirit; intelligence |
| **lèstoma** | *n.* belly; stomach |
| **li** | *pro.* he; she; it |
| **liméro/niméro** | *n.* number |
| **limon** | *n.* lemon |
| **(la)limyær** | *n.* light |
| **lindi** | *n.* Monday |
| **linèt** | *n.* glasses |
| **linj** | *n.* clothes |
| **linmé, linm** | *v.* love; like |
| **(la)linn** | *n.* moon |
| **linstrumen** | *n.* musical instrument |
| **lir** | *v.* read |
| **lis** | *n.* list |
| **listwar** | *n.* story |
| **lit** | *n.* bed |
| **liv** | *n.* book; pound (unit of measurement) |
| **livær** | *n.* winter |
| **lofis** | *n.* office |
| **lonch** | *n.* lunch |
| **lontem** | *adv.* long time |
| **lontem pasé** | *advphr.* long time ago |
| **lopital** | *n.* hospital |
| **lotòn** | *n.* autumn; fall |
| **(la)lotri** | *n.* lottery |
| **lòragan** | *n.* hurricane; storm |
| **lòt** | *adj.* other |
| **lœr** | *n.* hour; o'clock |
| **loué, lou** | *v.* rent |
| **lougarou** | *n.* werewolf |
| **fé lougarou** | *vphr.* stay out late gallivanting |
| **lour** | *adj.* heavy |
| **louvraj** | *n.* work |
| **lwil** | *n.* oil |
| **lwin** | *adv, prep.* far |
| **(La)Lwizyann** | *n.* Louisiana |

# M – m

| | |
|---|---|
| **madamm** | *n.* Mrs.; ma'am; lady; wife |
| **mal** | *n.* evil |
| **fé mal** | *vphr.* hurt |
| **malad** | *adj.* sick |
| **maléré** | *adj.* poor; unfortunate; sad |
| **malèrèzmen** | *adv.* unfortunately |
| **malgré** | *adv.* although |
| **malin** | *adj.* clever; sly |
| **mal-lagòrj/mal-de-gòrj** | *nphr.* sore throat |
| **mal-latèt/mal-de-tèt** | *nphr.* headache |
| **mal-o-den** | *n.* toothache |
| **mal-o-do** | *n.* backache |
| **mal-o-kœr** | *n.* heartburn |
| **mal-o-vent** | *n.* stomach ache |

| | |
|---|---|
| **mal-zòrèy** | *n.* earache |
| **mandé, mand** | *v.* ask |
| **manjé** | *n.* food |
| **manjé, manj** | *v.* eat |
| **manké, mank** | *v.* miss; almost do something |
| **mardi** | *n.* Tuesday |
| **marènn** | *n.* godmother |
| **mari** | *n.* husband |
| **maringwin** | *n.* mosquito |
| **mariyé, mari** | *v.* marry |
| **maron** | *adj.* brown |
| **mars** | *n.* March |
| **marshé, marsh** | *v.* walk |
| **maryaj** | *n.* marriage |
| **mashinn** | *n.* machine; motor |
| **mayi** | *n.* corn |
| **mær** | *n.* mother |
| **(la)mær** | *n.* ocean |
| **mærkrédi** | *n.* Wednesday |
| **Mærkrédi-dê-Sònn** | *nphr.* Ash Wednesday |
| **mærsi** | *interj.* thanks |
| **menti, men** | *v.* lie |
| **mé** | *conj.* but |
| **mé** | *n.* May |
| **médsinn** | *n.* medicine |
| **méli-mélanj** | *n.* mix |
| **mélé, mèl** | *v.* mix |
| **fé (sô) ménaj** | *vphr.* do one's chores |
| **ménajé, ménaj** | *v.* use sparingly; economize |
| **mérikin** | *adj., n.* American; English language |
| **Mérikin** | *n.* American person |
| **métrès** | *nphr.* teacher (female) |
| **méyœr** | *adj.* better; best |
| **(la)mézon** | *n.* house |
| **ménné, mènn** | *v.* bring; haul |
| **ménné/fé lembara** | *vphr.* cause trouble |
| **(la)mès** | *n.* church; mass |
| **mèsi** | *interj.* thanks |
| **mèt** | *v.* put; put on |
| **mèt-(d)-lékol/mèt** | *nphr.* teacher (male) |
| **midi** | *adv.* noon |
| **mil** | *n.* thousand; mile |
| **milé** | *n.* mule |
| **(la)min** | *n.* hand |
| **minm** | *adj.* same; even |
| **-minm** | *reflexive* (see Grammar Sketch, p. 98) |
| **minn** | *v.* mean |
| **mir** | *adj.* ripe |
| **(dé)mir** | *n.* berry |
| **(la)miray** | *n.* wall |
| **misyé** | *n.* Mr.; sir; gentleman |
| **(la)mizær** | *n.* misery; trouble |
| **(la)mizik** | *n.* music |
| **mizisyin** | *n.* musician |
| **(dé)mlon** | *n.* melon |
| **mo** | *pro.* I (subject) |
| **moman** | *n.* mom |
| **montañ** | *n.* mountain |
| **monté, mont** | *v.* ride |
| **montré, mont** | *v.* teach; show |
| **movè** | *adj.* bad |
| **mò** | *pro.* me (object) |
| **(la)mòché** | *n.* half of |
| **mòché-fræ r** | *n.* half-brother |
| **mòché-sœr** | *n.* half-sister |
| **mòr** | *adj.* dead |
| **(la)mòr** | *n.* death |
| **mòrd** | *v.* bite; sting |
| **mòrso** | *n.* little piece |
| **mòyær** | *n, adv.* way (of doing); kind of |
| **moun** | *n.* person |
| **mouri** | *v.* die |
| **moustash** | *n.* mustache |
| **(dé)moush** | *n.* fly |
| **moush-a-myèl** | *n.* honeybee |
| **(la)moutard** | *n.* mustard |
| **mouton** | *n.* sheep |
| **mouyé, mouy** | *v.* wet; rain |
| **mwins** | *adv, n.* less |
| **myé** | *adj.* better |
| **mô** | *det.* my |

# N – n

| | |
|---|---|
| **najé, naj** | *v.* swim |
| **nanglé** | *n.* English language |
| **namm** | *n.* soul |
| **napa** | *n.* bait |
| **narb** | *n.* tree |
| **natirèl** | *adj.* natural |
| **né** | *v.* born |
| **néjé, nèj** | *v.* snow |
| **népi-mayi** | *nphr.* ear of corn |
| **névé** | *n.* nephew |
| **nèf, nœf** | *n.* nine |
| **(la)nèj** | *n.* snow |
| **nètwayé, nètwa** | *v.* clean |
| **nidé** | *n.* idea; mind; thought |
| **nik** | *n.* nest |
| **nimpòrt éyou** | *nphr.* anywhere |
| **nimpòrt ki moun** | *nphr.* anybody |
| **nimpòrt ki plas** | *nphr.* anywhere |
| **nimpòrt ki zafær** | *nphr.* anything |
| **nimpòrt kishòj** | *nphr.* anything |
| **nimpòrt (ki)** | *adj, n.* any; whatever; whichever |
| **nivo** | *n.* level |
| **nom** | *n.* name |
| **nom-d-famiy** | *n.* surname |
| **nom-d-maryaj** | *n.* married name |
| **non** | *interj.* no |
| **non pli** | *adv.* anymore; either |
| **nonk** | *n.* uncle |
| **nonm** | *n.* man |
| **nora** | *vphr.* there will be |
| **novemb** | *n.* November |
| **no, nouzòt** | *pro.* we (subject) |
| **nòr** | *n, adj.* north |
| **nòtis** | *n.* sign |
| **Nouvèl-Òrléan** | *n.* New Orleans |
| **nouvo** | *adj.* new |
| **nou, nouzòt** | *pro.* us (object) |
| **nwa** | *n.* nut |
| **nwaj** | *n.* cloud |
| **nwar** | *adj.* black |
| **nwayé, nway** | *v.* drown |
| **Nwèl** | *n.* Christmas |
| **(la)nwit** | *n.* night |
| **nyès** | *n.* niece |
| **nô** | *det.* our |

# O – o

| | |
|---|---|
| **obòr isit** | *prep.* around here |
| **ofon** | *prep.* the bottom |
| **okipé** | *adj.* busy |
| **oktòb** | *n.* October |
| **olé** | *v.* want |
| **(l)ombraj** | *n.* shade |
| **omwin** | *conj.* at least |
| **onz** | *n.* eleven |
| **opré** | *prep.* nearby |
| **ora** | *prep.* near; around |
| **orévwar** | *interj.* goodbye |
| **osike** | *advphr.* as soon as |
| **osit** | *conj.* also; too |
| **osi...ke** | *adjphr.* as...as |
| **oté, ot** | *v.* take off; remove |
| **Ozilinwa** | *n.* Illinois |

# OU – ou

| | |
|---|---|
| **ou** | *conj.* or |
| **ouvraj** | *n.* work |
| **ouvri, ouvær** | *v.* open |

# P – p

| | |
|---|---|
| **pa** | *conj.* negative marker; not |
| **pa ditou** | *adv.* not at all |
| **pa enkòr** | *adv.* not yet |
| **pa gran-shòj** | *adv.* not much |
| **pa nil-plas** | *adv.* nowhere |
| **pa-d-kwa** | *phr.* you're welcome |
| **padna** | *n.* friend |
| **Pak** | *n.* Easter |
| **pakònn** | *n.* pecan |
| **pantalon** | *n.* pants |
| **par ègzamp** | *exp.* for example |
| **paradi** | *n.* heaven |
| **pardonné, pardonn** | *v.* forgive |
| **paren** | *n.* parent; relative |
| **paré** | *adj.* ready |
| **parésé** | *adj.* lazy |
| **paréy** | *adj.* same; similar |
| **parin** | *n.* godfather |
| **parlé, parl** | *v.* speak |
| **paròl** | *n.* word |
| **parske** | *conj.* because |
| **partajé, partaj** | *v.* share |
| **parti, par** | *v.* leave |
| **pasé** | *adv.* ago |
| **pasé, pas** | *v.* pass; pass away |
| **(la)pat** | *n.* paw; leg or foot (of animal) |
| **patasa** | *n.* sunfish |
| **patat** | *n.* potato; sweet potato |
| **patat dous** | *n.* sweet potato |
| **patouyé, patouy** | *v.* splash around |
| **pay** | *n.* pie |
| **(la)pay** | *n.* straw; husk |
| **pær** | *n.* father |
| **pærd** | *v.* lose |
| **pærdi** | *adj.* lost |
| **(pa) pærsonn** | *n.* no one |
| **pe** | *v.* able to; can |
| **pendan** | *conj.* during; while |
| **penn** | *v.* hang |
| **pensé, pens** | *v.* think |
| **petèt** | *adv.* maybe |
| **pé** | *v.* shut up; quiet |
| **pélikan** | *n.* pelican |
| **pélé, pèl** | *v.* call; be named (reflexive) |
| **pèshé, pèsh** | *v.* prevent; fish; sin |
| **péshœr** | *n.* fisher; sinner |
| **péyé, péy** | *v.* pay |
| **péyi** | *n.* country; nation |
| **pèlé, pèl** | *v.* call; be named (reflexive) |
| **pèshé, pèsh** | *v.* prevent; fish; sin |
| **pi** | *conj.* then |
| **pikan** | *n.* sticker; thorn |
| **pimen** | *n.* pepper (vegetable) |
| **pimenté** | *v, adj.* spice; spicy; spiced |
| **pipi** | *v, n.* pee |
| **piti** | *adj.* small; little |
| **piti** | *n.* child |
| **pla** | *n.* plate; dish (of food) |

| | |
|---|---|
| **plakminn** | *n.* persimmon |
| **planshé** | *n.* floor |
| **plant** | *n.* plant |
| **planté, plant** | *v.* plant |
| **plas** | *n.* place; space |
| **play** | *n.* beach |
| **pléri** | *n.* prairie |
| **plézir** | *n.* pleasure |
| **plènn** | *n.* plain |
| **pli(s)** | *adv, n.* more |
| **(la)pli** | *n.* rain |
| **plin** | *adj, n.* full; a lot |
| **plizyær** | *adj.* many |
| **pli...ke** | *adjphr.* more...than |
| **(la)plòt** | *n.* ball |
| **(la)po** | *n.* skin |
| **pokapok** | *adj.* so-so |
| **polis** | *n.* police |
| **popa** | *n.* dad |
| **(ré)pozé, (ré)poz** | *v.* rest; relax (sometimes reflexive) |
| **pòrt** | *n.* door |
| **pòrté, pòrt** | *v.* bring; wear |
| **pòrtré** | *n.* picture; photo; movie |
| **gin pœr** | *vphr.* afraid |
| **pœr** | *n, v.* fear; afraid |
| **pou** | *prep.* for; about; to |
| **pou sûr** | *advphr.* for sure; definitely |
| **(la)poud** | *n.* powder; dust; gunpowder |
| **poul** | *n.* chicken; hen |
| **poulayé** | *n.* henhouse |
| **pousé, pous** | *v.* push; grow |
| **(la)pousyær** | *n.* dust |
| **prenn** | *v.* take |
| **pré** | *prep.* near; close |
| **prèmyé** | *adj.* first |
| **prèsk** | *adj, adv.* almost |
| **printem** | *n.* spring |
| **priyé, priy** | *v.* pray |
| **prizon** | *n.* prison |
| **promèt** | *v.* promise |
| **proshin** | *adj.* next |
| **protéjé, protèj** | *v.* protect |
| **pròsh** | *adj, adv.* near; nearly; almost |
| **pur** | *adj.* pure |
| **(dé)pwa** | *n.* green peas |
| **(la)pwal** | *n.* frying pan |
| **(dé)pwar** | *n.* pear |
| **pwason** | *n.* fish |
| **pwason-armé** | *n.* gar (fish) |
| **pyas** | *n.* dollar |
| **pyé** | *n.* foot |
| **pyoshé, pyòsh** | *v.* hoe; dig |

# R – r

| | |
|---|---|
| **ra** | *n.* rat |
| **ra-d-bwa** | *n.* possum |
| **ramasé, ramas** | *v.* gather; pick up; collect |
| **ranjé, ranj** | *v.* fix; repair; arrange; prepare |
| **raplé, rapèl** | *v.* remember |
| **rar** | *adj.* rare |
| **(la)ras** | *n.* race |
| **ravé** | *n.* cockroach |
| **rentré, rent** | *v.* enter; return; come home |
| **rékòlt** | *n.* harvest; crop |
| **fé rékòlt** | *vphr.* farm |
| **réméd** | *n.* remedy; medicine |
| **réponn** | *v.* answer; respond |
| **répons** | *n.* answer; response |
| **gin rézon** | *vphr/adjphr.* right |
| **rèspé** | *n.* respect |

| | |
|---|---|
| **rèspèkté, rèspèk** | *v.* respect |
| **rèsté, rès** | *v.* stay; remain; habitate; live; dwell |
| **rèshté, rèshèt** | *v.* vomit; throw up |
| **rèv** | *n.* dream |
| **rèvé, rèv** | *v.* dream |
| **(la)rimm** | *n.* cold (sickness); flu |
| **(la)rivyær** | *n.* river |
| **rodayé, roday** | *v.* travel on the road; roam; gallivant |
| **rodayœr** | *n.* traveller |
| **roti** | *v.* roast; grill |
| **roz** | *adj.* pink |
| **(la)rozé** | *n.* dew |
| **ròb** | *n.* dress |
| **rouyé** | *adj.* rusted; rusty |

# S – s

| | |
|---|---|
| **sa** | *aux.* future marker; will be |
| **safré, saf** | *v.* eat (of animals); eat like an animal (of humans) |
| **(la)sal** | *n.* room |
| **sal** | *adj.* dirty |
| **(la)salad** | *n.* salad |
| **sal-a-manjé** | *n.* dining room |
| **salé** | *v, adj.* salt; salted |
| **sali** | *v.* get dirty |
| **salon** | *n.* living room |
| **Sammdi Sin** | *nphr.* Holy Saturday |
| **san** | *conj.* without |
| **sanmdi** | *n.* Saturday |
| **sasafra** | *n.* sassafras |
| **fé særmen** | *vphr.* swear |
| **særmen** | *n.* swear; promise |
| **særvi, sær** | *v.* use |
| **senm** | *v.* seem; appear; look like |
| **senti, sen** | *v.* feel (reflexive); smell |
| **sé** | *aux.* conditional marker; would be |
| **séyé, séy** | *v.* try |
| **(la)sézon** | *n.* season |
| **sézonné, sézonn** | *v, adj.* season; seasoned |
| **sèk** | *adj.* dry |
| **sèptemb** | *n.* September |
| **sèt** | *n.* seven |
| **sèz** | *n.* sixteen |
| **si** | *conj.* if; so |
| **si tèlmen** | *adv.* so (to emphasize an adjective); so much; so many |
| **sid** | *n, adj.* south |
| **sidès** | *n, adj.* southeast |
| **siflé, sif** | *v.* whistle |
| **singgo** | *n, v.* nap |
| **sinkant** | *n.* fifty |
| **sinkant-é-ènn** | *n.* fifty-one |
| **sinmé, sinm** | *v.* sow |
| **siñ** | *n.* sign |
| **fé siñ lakrwa** | *vphr.* cross oneself |
| **sipozé (pou)** | *aux.* supposed to |
| **sipozé, sipòz** | *v.* suppose |
| **sipré** | *n.* Eastern red cedar |
| **sipriyær** | *n.* swamp; cypress swamp |
| **sirkonflèks** | *n.* circumflex (accent mark) |
| **siro** | *n.* syrup; womanizer |
| **sis** | *n.* six |
| **sisé, sis** | *v.* suck |
| **sitoplé, sivouplé** | *interj.* please |
| **smat** | *adj.* smart |
| **(la)smènn** | *n.* week |
| **so** | *interj.* so (discourse particle) |
| **sofa** | *n.* sofa; couch |
| **sol** | *n.* willow tree |
| **soléy** | *n.* sun |
| **soléy-koushé** | *n.* sunset |
| **soléy-lévé** | *n.* sunrise |
| **sosis** | *n.* sausage |

| | |
|---|---|
| **fé sosyété** | *vphr.* throw a party |
| **sové, sov** | *v.* save |
| **sòrti salé** | *vphr.* turn out bad |
| **sòrti, sòr** | *v.* be from (somewhere); go out; end up |
| **(la)sòs** | *n.* sauce |
| **sòt** | *adj.* foolish |
| **spañol** | *adj., n.* Spanish |
| **Spañol** | *n.* Spanish person |
| **spéré, èspær** | *v.* wait |
| **spìnn** | *v.* spin records |
| **sœl** | *adj.* alone |
| **sœr** | *n.* sister |
| **sou** | *n.* cent |
| **souflé, souf** | *v.* blow (of wind); breathe |
| **soulyé** | *n.* shoes |
| **(la)soup** | *n.* soup |
| **soupé** | *n.* supper |
| **soutærin** | *n.* basement |
| **souven** | *adv.* often |
| **stìl** | *adv.* still |
| **sto** | *n.* store |
| **stov** | *n.* stove |
| **supærb** | *adj.* super; wonderful |
| **sur** | *prep.* on |
| **surtou** | *adv.* especially |
| **swaf** | *adj.* thirsty |
| **swaré** | *n.* evening; eveningtime |
| **swasant** | *n.* sixty |
| **swasant-dis** | *n.* seventy |
| **swasant-é-ènn** | *n.* sixty-one |
| **swasant-onz** | *n.* seventy-one |
| **swaté, swat** | *v.* hope; wish |
| **swé** | *v.* sweat |
| **swiv** | *v.* follow |
| **swonñé, swonñ** | *v.* care for; nurse |
| **syèl** | *n.* sky; heaven |
| **sô** | *det.* his; her; its |
| **fé sô nidé** | *vphr.* make up one's mind |
| **sur** | *prep.* on |
| **sûr** | *adj.* sure; certain |

# SH – sh

| | |
|---|---|
| **shagrin** | *adj.* sorry; sad |
| **shak** | *adj.* each; every; shucks |
| **shandèl** | *n.* candle |
| **shanjé, shanj** | *v.* change |
| **shanm** | *n.* room; bedroom |
| **shanm-a-bin** | *n.* bathroom |
| **shanm-a-koushé** | *n.* bedroom |
| **(la)shans** | *n.* luck; chance |
| **shanson** | *n.* song |
| **shanté, shant** | *v.* sing |
| **shapé, shap** | *v.* escape; get away |
| **shapo** | *n.* hat |
| **shar** | *n.* car |
| **sharé, shar** | *v.* chat |
| **sharshé, sharsh** | *v.* seek; look for |
| **shasé, shas** | *v.* hunt |
| **shawi** | *n.* raccoon |
| **shær** | *adj.* expensive; dear |
| **shevrèt** | *n.* shrimp |
| **shé** | *prep.* at the home of |
| **shévé** | *n.* hair |
| **shèvréy** | *n.* deer |
| **shiké, shik** | *v.* chew |
| **shimij** | *n.* shirt |
| **shmin** | *n.* road; path |
| **sho** | *adj.* hot |
| **shodyær** | *n.* pot; pan |
| **shoké** | *adj.* mad; angry |
| **(dé)shou** | *n.* cabbage |
| **shval** | *n.* horse |
| **shyin** | *n.* dog |

# T – t

| | |
|---|---|
| **(la)tab** | *n.* table |
| **taba** | *n.* tobacco |
| **taktak** | *n.* popcorn |
| **talœr** | *adv.* soon |
| **tambou** | *n.* drum |
| **tan** | *adj, adv.* so many; so |
| **tandi** | *conj.* while |
| **tanpri** | *interj.* please |
| **tant** | *n.* aunt |
| **tar** | *adj.* late |
| **tas** | *n.* cup |
| **tayé, tay** | *v.* beat |
| **(la)tær** | *n.* earth; ground; dirt |
| **tem** | *n.* weather; time |
| **tem-zen-tem** | *adv.* now and then; occasionally |
| **tendé, tenn** | *v.* hear |
| **té** | *aux.* past marker; was |
| **Tèksas** | *n.* Texas |
| **tèl** | *adj.* such |
| **tèl-é-tèl** | *nphr.* such and such |
| **(la)tèt** | *n.* head |
| **ti** | *n.* small; little |
| **ti brin** | *nphr.* a little |
| **ti-bétay** | *nphr.* insect; bug |
| **ti-fiy** | *n.* granddaughter |
| **tig** | *n.* tiger |
| **ti-garçon** | *n.* grandson |
| **tikèt** | *n.* ticket |
| **ti-nom** | *n.* nickname |
| **tiyon** | *n.* headscarf; tignon |
| **(la)tizann** | *n.* herbal tea |
| **ti-zenfan, ti-piti** | *n.* grandchild |
| **to** | *pro.* you (subject) |
| **tomat** | *n.* tomato |
| **tombé, tomb** | *v.* fall |
| **tònær** | *n.* thunder |
| **tòrné, tòrn** | *v.* turn |
| **tou** | *adj.* all |
| **tou alentour** | *prep.* all around |
| **toujou** | *adj, adv.* always; still |
| **toukèkunn** | *nphr.* everyone; everybody |
| **toukishòj** | *n.* everything |
| **toulajourné** | *adv.* all day long |
| **toulédé** | *n.* both |
| **touléjour** | *adv.* every day |
| **toultem** | *adv.* forever; always |
| **toumoun** | *nphr.* everyone |
| **gin toupé** | *vphr.* have nerve |
| **tous** | *n.* cough |
| **Tou-Sin** | *nphr.* All Saints Day |
| **tousé, tous** | *v.* cough |
| **tousœl** | *adj., adv.* all alone |
| **traka** | *n.* problem; trouble |
| **trakasé, trakas** | *v.* worry |
| **trankil** | *adj.* peaceful; quiet; calm |
| **trapé, trap** | *v.* get; catch; trap |
| **travay** | *n.* work |
| **travayé, travay** | *v.* work |
| **trent** | *n.* thirty |
| **trent-é-ènn** | *n.* thirty-one |
| **trézòr** | *n.* treasure |
| **trènné, trènn** | *v.* trail; drag |
| **trèz** | *n.* thirteen |
| **fé trin** | *vphr.* complain |
| **trin** | *n.* noise; train |
| **tris** | *adj.* sad |
| **tro** | *adj.* too |
| **tro bokou** | *nphr.* too many; too much |
| **trò** | *n.* three |
| **tròk** | *n.* truck |
| **tròs** | *v.* trust |
| **twa** | *n.* roof |
| **twa** | *pro.* you (object) |
| **twalèt** | *n.* dresser |
| **tô** | *det.* your (singular) |

# V – v

| | |
|---|---|
| **va** | *aux.* future marker (see Grammar Sketch); will |
| **vash** | *n.* cow |
| **vayan** | *adj.* great; excellent; nice |
| **vær** | *adj.* green |
| **vær** | *n.* glass; glass (for drinking) |
| **(dé)vær** | *n.* worm |
| **ve** | *v.* want |
| **vendrédi** | *n.* Friday |
| **Vendrédi Sin** | *nphr.* Good Friday |
| **venn** | *v.* sell |
| **vent** | *n.* stomach; belly |
| **(la)vésèl** | *n.* dishes |
| **(la)vi** | *n.* life |
| **vid** | *adj.* empty |
| **vidyo** | *n.* video |
| **(la)vil** | *n.* city |
| **vilaj** | *n.* town |
| **vilin** | *adj.* mean; nasty; ugly |
| **vin** | *n.* twenty |
| **vin-dé** | *n.* twenty-two |
| **vinég** | *n.* vinegar |
| **vini, vyin** | *v.* come; become |
| **vint-é-ènn** | *n.* twenty-one |
| **vit** | *adj, adv.* fast; quickly |
| **viv** | *v.* live; dwell |
| **vivan** | *adj.* living; alive |
| **vizité, vizit** | *v.* visit (person or place) |
| **vo** | *v.* worth |
| **vo myé** | *vphr.* prefer; would be better |
| **volé, vòl** | *v.* fly; steal |
| **vomi** | *v.* vomit |
| **voyé, vòy** | *v.* send; throw |
| **vou** | *pro.* you (plural; formal) (subject and object) |
| **vré** | *adj.* true |
| **(la)vwa** | *n.* voice |
| **vwala** | *interj.* voilà |
| **vwayaj** | *n.* voyage; trip |
| **vwayajé, vwayaj** | *v.* travel |
| **vwazin** | *n.* neighbor (male or female) |
| **vwazinaj** | *n.* neighborhood; vicinity |
| **vwazinn** | *n.* neighbor (female) |
| **(la)vyann** | *n.* meat |
| **vyé** | *adj.* old |
| **vyolèt** | *n, adj.* violet (flower); violet (color) |
| **vô** | *det.* your (polite) |

# W – w

| | |
|---|---|
| **war** | *v.* see |
| **wawaron** | *n.* bullfrog |
| **wèl** | *interj.* well (discourse particle) |
| **wès** | *n, adj.* west |
| **wi** | *interj.* yes |
| **wiski** | *n.* whiskey |
| **wit** | *n.* eight |

# Y – y

| | |
|---|---|
| **yær** | *adv.* yesterday |
| **yé** | *pro.* they (subject and object) |
| **-yé** | *det.* plural marker |
| **yéyay!** | *interj.* yeyaille!; wow! |
| **yê** | *v.* be (interrogative); be (relative) |
| **yê** | *det.* their |

# Z – z

| | |
|---|---|
| **zafær** | *n.* thing |
| **zan** | *n.* year (when counting or with a number) |
| **fé zan** | *vphr.* turn (an age) |
| **zariko** | *n, adj.* beans; zydeco |
| **zartik** | *n.* article |
| **zaryin** | *n.* spider |
| **zærb** | *n.* grass |
| **zen (dê)** | *adjphr.* some |
| **zégré** | *n.* egret |
| **zéklær** | *n.* lightning |
| **zépol** | *n.* shoulder |
| **zétaj** | *n.* floor (of a building) |
| **(dé)zèf** | *n.* egg |
| **zindyin** | *n, adj.* Indian (Native American) |
| **(dé)zo** | *n.* bone |
| **zoranj** | *n, adj.* orange (fruit); orange (color) |
| **zònyon** | *n.* onion |
| **zòrèy** | *n.* ear |
| **zòrtèy** | *n.* toe |
| **(vou)zòt** | *pro.* you (plural) (subject and object) |
| **(dé)zòt** | *n.* others |
| **zœr** | *n.* hour; o'clock |
| **zouti** | *n.* tool |
| **(dé)zwa** | *n.* goose |
| **zwazo** | *n.* bird |
| **(dé)zwit** | *n.* oyster |
| **zyé** | *n.* eye |
| **fé zyé dou(apré)** | *vphr.* make eyes (at) |

# Lexicon

*English–Creole*

## A – a

| | |
|---|---|
| **a little** | *n.* in pe |
| | *nphr.* ti brin |
| **a lot** | *nphr.* in ta |
| | *adj, n.* plin |
| **a while** | *nphr.* bout-d-tem |
| **a(n)** | *n.* in |
| **able** | *aux.* kapab |
| | *v.* koné |
| **able to** | *v.* pe |
| **about** | *prep.* alentour |
| | *prep.* pou |
| **above** | *prep.* enho |
| | *adv, adj.* enlær |
| **act of meeting someone** | |
| | *n.* (la)kònésans |
| **Advent** | *n.* Lavonn |
| **advice** | *n.* konsèy |
| **afraid** | *n, v.* pœr |
| | *vphr.* gin pœr |

| | |
|---|---|
| **African** | *n, adj.* Afrikin; afrikin |
| **after** | *adv, prep.* apré |
| **afternoon** | *nphr.* aprémidi |
| **age** | *n.* (l)aj |
| **ago** | *adv.* pasé |
| **agreed** | *interj, n, adj.* dakòr |
| **airplane** | *n.* batimen-d-ær |
| | *n.* éroplènn |
| **alive** | *adj.* vivan |
| **all** | *adj.* tou |
| **all around** | *prep.* tou alentour |
| **all day long** | *adv.* toulajourné |
| **All Saints Day** | *nphr.* la Tou-Sin |
| **alligator** | *n.* kokodri |
| **allowed to** | *vphr.* gin drwa |
| **almost** | *adj, adv.* prèsk |
| | *adj, adv.* pròsh |
| **almost do something** *v.* manké, mank | |
| **alone** | *adj.* sèl |

| | |
|---|---|
| **alphabet** | *n.* alfabèt |
| **also** | *conj.* itou |
| | *conj.* osit |
| **although** | *conj.* kanminm |
| | *adv.* malgré |
| **always** | *adj, adv.* toujou |
| | *adv.* toultem |
| **Amen** | *phr.* Insiswatil |
| **American** | *adj., n.* mérikin |
| **American person** | *n.* Mérikin |
| **and** | *conj.* é |
| | *conj.* épi |
| **andouille (sausage)** | *n.* (l)andoui |
| **anger** | *n, adj.* kolær |
| **angry** | *n, adj.* kolær |
| | *adj.* shoké |
| **animal** | *adj, n.* bèt |
| **animal feed** | *n.* fid |
| **annoy** | *v, adj.* enmærdé, enmærd |
| **another** | *prep.* in lòt/in nòt |
| **answer** | *v.* réponn |
| | *n.* répons |
| **any** | *adj, n.* nimpòrt (ki) |
| **anybody** | *nphr.* nimpòrt ki moun |
| **anymore** | *adv.* non pli |
| **anything** | *nphr.* nimpòrt kishòj |
| | *nphr.* nimpòrt ki zafær |
| **anywhere** | *nphr.* nimpòrt éyou |
| | *nphr.* nimpòrt ki plas |
| **appear** | *vphr.* gin lè |
| | *v.* senm |
| **approximately** | *prep.* alentour |
| **April** | *n.* avril |
| **arm** | *n.* bra |
| **around** | *prep.* alentour |
| | *prep.* ora |
| **around here** | *prep.* obòr isit |
| **arrange** | *v.* ranjé, ranj |
| **arrive** | *v.* arivé, ariv |
| **article** | *n.* zartik |
| **as soon as** | *advphr.* osike |
| **as...as** | *adjphr.* osi...ke |
| **Ash Wednesday** | *nphr.* Mærkrédi dê Senn |
| **ask** | *v.* mandé, mand |
| **at** | *prep.* a |
| | *prep.* koté |
| **at least** | *conj.* omwin |
| **at the home of** | *prep.* shé |
| **August** | *n.* aout |
| **aunt** | *n.* tant |
| **autumn** | *n.* lotòn |
| **awake** | *adj, adv.* débout |
| **awkward** | *adj.* gosh |
| **axe** | *n.* (la)hash |

# B – b

| | |
|---|---|
| **back** | *adj.* bæk |
| **backache** | *n.* mal-o-do |
| **bad** | *adj.* movὲ |
| **bad weather** | *n.* gro tem/movè tem |
| **bait** | *n.* napa |
| **ball** | *n.* (la)plòt |
| **banjo** | *n.* banndjo |
| **bank** | *n.* (la)bank |
| **barbed wire** | *n.* fil-a-kroshé |
| **bark** | *v.* japé, jap |
| **basement** | *n.* (la)kav |
| | *n.* soutærin |
| **basically** | *adv.* jolimen |
| **bathe** | *v.* bèñé, bèñ |
| **bathroom** | *n.* shanm-a-bin |
| **bayou** | *n.* bayou |
| **be** | *v.* çé |
| **be (imperative)** | *v.* dèt |
| **be (infinitive)** | *v.* dèt |
| **be (interrogative)** | *v.* yê |
| **be (relative)** | *v.* yê |
| **be careful** | *phr.* fé atensyon |
| **be from (somewhere)** | *v.* sòrti, sòr |
| **beach** | *n.* play |

| | |
|---|---|
| **bead** | *n.* biy |
| **beans** | *n, adj.* zariko |
| **beard** | *n.* (la)barb |
| **beat** | *v.* bat |
| | *v.* tayé, tay |
| **beautiful** | *adj.* bèl |
| | *adj.* joli |
| **because** | *conj.* akoz |
| | *conj.* parske |
| **become** | *v.* vini, vyin |
| **bed** | *n.* lit |
| **bedroom** | *n.* shanm |
| | *n.* shanm-a-koushé |
| **beer** | *n.* (la)byær |
| **before** | *adv.* avan |
| **begin** | *v.* komensé, komens |
| **behind** | *prep.* dæryær |
| | *prep.* ennaryær |
| **beignet** | *n.* béñé |
| **believe** | *v.* krò |
| **belly** | *n.* lèstoma |
| | *n.* vent |
| **below** | *prep.* enba |
| **berry** | *n.* (dé)mir |
| **best** | *adj.* méyœr |
| **better** | *adj.* méyœr |
| | *adj.* myé |
| **Bible** | *n.* (La)Bib |
| **bicycle** | *n.* bisik |
| **big** | *adj.* gran |
| | *adj.* gro |
| **bird** | *n.* zwazo |
| **birthday** | *n.* (la)fèt |
| **bite** | *v.* mòrd |
| **bitter** | *adj.* anmær |
| **black** | *adj.* nwar |
| **block** | *v.* baré, bar |
| **blood** | *n.* disan |
| **bloom** | *v.* flèri |
| **blouse** | *n.* jozé |
| **blow (of wind)** | *v.* souflé, souf |
| **boat** | *n.* bato |
| **boil** | *v.* bouyi, bouy |

| | |
|---|---|
| **bone** | *n.* (dé)zo |
| **book** | *n.* liv |
| **boots** | *n.* bòt |
| **bored** | *adj.* ennwiyé |
| **born** | *v.* né |
| **boss** | *n.* bòs |
| **both** | *n.* toulédé |
| **bother** | *v, adj.* embarasé |
| **bottle** | *n.* boutéy |
| **boucherie** | *n.* (la)boushri |
| **boudin (sausage)** | *n.* boudin |
| **bowl** | *n.* bòl |
| **box** | *n.* bwat |
| **boy** | *n.* garçon |
| **boyfriend** | *n.* (l)amourè |
| | *n, adj.* kalin |
| **bread** | *n.* dipin |
| **break** | *v.* kasé, kas |
| **breakfast** | *n, v.* déjœné, déjœn |
| **breathe** | *v.* souflé, souf |
| **breeze** | *n.* (la)frèsh |
| **bring** | *v.* mènné, mènn |
| | *v.* pòrté, pòrt |
| **broom** | *n.* balé |
| **brother** | *n.* fræр |
| **brother-in-law** | *n.* bo-fræр |
| **brown** | *adj.* maron |
| **buckle** | *v.* bouklé, bouk |
| **bug** | *nphr.* ti-bétay |
| **build** | *v.* bati |
| **building** | *n.* batis |
| **bullfrog** | *n.* wawaron |
| **bump** | *v.* koñé, koñ |
| **burn** | *v.* brilé, bril |
| | *n.* brilmen |
| **busy** | *adj.* okipé |
| **but** | *conj.* mé |
| **butt** | *n.* bounda |
| | *n.* chi |
| | *n.* gogo |
| **butter** | *n.* dibœr |
| **buy** | *v.* ashté, ashèt |
| **buzzard** | *n.* karankro |

# C – c

| | |
|---|---|
| **cabbage** | *n.* (dé)shou |
| **Cajun** | *n., adj.* kadjin |
| **Cajun person** | *n.* Kadjin |
| **cake** | *n.* kék |
| **cake (general)** | *n.* gato |
| **call** | *v.* pélé, pèl |
| **calm** | *adj.* trankil |
| **can** | *aux.* kapab |
| | *v.* koné |
| | *v.* pe |
| **candle** | *n.* shandèl |
| **captain** | *n.* kapitènn |
| **car** | *n.* shar |
| **card** | *n.* kart |
| **care for** | *v.* swonñé, swonñ |
| **Carencro** | *n.* karankro |
| **carrot** | *n.* karòt |
| **catch** | *v.* trapé, trap |
| **catfish** | *n.* barbi |
| **Catholic** | *n, adj.* Katolik |
| **cause trouble** | *vphr.* fé kòmærs |
| | *vphr.* mènné/fé lembara |
| **cent** | *n.* sou |
| **certain** | *adj.* sûr |
| **challenge** | *n.* défi |
| **chamomile** | *n.* kammòmèl |
| **chance** | *n.* (la)shans |
| **change** | *v.* shanjé, shanj |
| **change suddenly** | *v.* boulværsé, boulværs |
| **chat** | *v.* kozé, kòz |
| | *v.* sharé, shar |
| **chatter** | *vphr.* galopé laboush |
| **cheap** | *adj.* bon-marshé |
| **check** | *v.* chéké, chèk |
| **cheese** | *n.* fromaj |
| **chew** | *v.* shiké, shik |
| **chicken** | *n.* poul |
| **child** | *n.* piti |
| **Christmas** | *n.* Krismis |
| | *n.* Nwèl |

| | |
|---|---|
| **church** | *n.* légliz |
| | *n.* (la)mès |
| **circumflex (accent mark)** | *n.* sirkonflèks |
| **city** | *n.* (la)vil |
| **clean** | *v.* nètwayé, nètwa |
| **clear** | *adj, adv.* klær |
| **clearly** | *adj, adv.* klær |
| | *adv.* klærmen |
| **clever** | *adj.* malin |
| **close** | *v.* færmé, færm |
| | *prep.* pré |
| **closet** | *n.* kabinèt |
| **clothes** | *n.* linj |
| **cloud** | *n.* nwaj |
| **cloudy** | *adj.* kouvær |
| **club** | *n.* klœb |
| **clumsy** | *adj.* gosh |
| **coat** | *n.* kapo |
| **cockroach** | *n.* ravé |
| **coffee** | *n.* kafé |
| **cold** | *adj.* frèt |
| **cold (sickness)** | *n.* (la)rimm |
| **collect** | *v.* ramasé, ramas |
| **color** | *n.* kouloer |
| **come** | *v.* vini, vyin |
| **come home** | *v.* rentré, rent |
| **company (people)** | *n.* (la)kompoñi |
| **complain** | *vphr.* fé trin |
| **complete** | *v.* fini |
| **conditional marker** | *aux.* sé |
| **continue** | *v.* kontiné |
| **conversation** | *n.* konværsasyon |
| **cook** | *v.* kwi |
| **cool** | *adj.* frèsh |
| **corn** | *n.* mayi |
| **cornbread with sugar and milk** | *n.* koushkoush |
| **corncob** | *n.* kòton-mayi |
| **cornstalk** | *nphr.* baton-mayi |
| **correct** | *adj.* kòrèk |

| | |
|---|---|
| **cost** | *v.* kouté, kout |
| **cottage cheese** | *n.* kayé |
| **cotton** | *n.* koton |
| **couch** | *n.* sofa |
| **cough** | *n.* tous |
| | *v.* tousé, tous |
| **country** | *n.* (la)kamponñ |
| | *n.* péyi |
| **countryside** | *n.* (la)kamponñ |
| **court** | *nphr.* fé lakour |
| **cousin (female)** | *n.* kouzinn |
| **cousin (male or female)** | *n.* kouzin |
| **covered** | *adj.* kouvær |
| **cow** | *n.* bèf |
| | *n.* vash |
| **crab** | *n.* krab |
| **crack** | *v.* kasé, kas |
| **crawfish** | *n.* krébis |
| **crazy** | *adj.* fou |
| **Creole** | *adj., n.* kréyòl |
| **Creole person** | *n.* Kréyòl |
| **crop** | *n.* rékòlt |
| **cross oneself** | *vphr.* fé siñ lakrwa |
| **cunning** | *adj.* kanay |
| **cup** | *n.* kòp |
| | *n.* tas |
| **cure** | *v.* géri |
| | *n.* gérison |
| **curious** | *adj.* kiriyé |
| **cut** | *v.* koupé, koup |
| **cypress knee** | *n.* boskoyo |
| **cypress swamp** | *n.* sipriyær |

## D – d

| | |
|---|---|
| **dad** | *n.* popa |
| **damage** | *n.* domaj |
| **dance** | *v.* dansé, dans |
| **dance (social gathering)** | *n.* bal |
| **dancehall** | *n.* hòl |
| **dark (of color)** | *adj.* fonsé |
| **date** | *nphr.* fé lakour |
| **daughter** | *n.* fiy |
| **daughter-in-law** | *n.* bèl-fiy |
| **day** | *n.* jour |
| | *n.* (la)journé |
| **daytime** | *n.* (la)journé |
| **dead** | *adj.* mòr |
| **dear** | *adj.* shær |
| **death** | *n.* (la)mòr |
| **December** | *n.* désemb |
| **deep** | *adj, n.* fon |
| **deer** | *n.* shèvréy |
| **definitely** | *advphr.* pou sûr |
| **depressed** | *adj.* dégouté |
| **depths** | *adj, n.* fon |
| **dew** | *n.* (la)rozé |
| **diarrhea** | *n.* (la)chirout |
| **die** | *v.* krévé, krèv |
| | *v.* mouri |
| **difference** | *n.* diférens |
| **different** | *adj.* diféren |
| **difficult** | *adj.* dur |
| **dig** | *v.* pyoshé, pyòsh |
| **dining room** | *n.* sal-a-manjé |
| **dirt** | *n.* (la)tær |
| **dirty** | *v.* barbouyé, barbouy |
| | *adj.* sal |
| **discourage** | *v, adj.* dékourajé |
| **discouraged** | *v, adj.* dékourajé |
| **disgusted** | *adj.* dégouté |
| **dish (of food)** | *n.* pla |
| **dishes** | *n.* (la)vésèl |
| **dislike** | *v.* détèsté, détès |
| **disorder** | *adj, n.* dézòrd |
| **do** | *v.* fé |
| **do one's chores** | *vphr.* fé (sô) ménaj |
| **do one's homework** | *vphr.* fé (sô) dévwa |
| **do regularly** | *aux.* koné |
| **do you..?** | *conj.* èske |
| **dog** | *n.* shyin |

| | | | |
|---|---|---|---|
| **dollar** | *n.* pyas | **drown** | *v.* nwayé, nway |
| **door** | *n.* pòrt | **drum** | *n.* tambou |
| **drag** | *v.* trènné, trènn | **drunk** | *adj.* chak |
| **dream** | *n.* rèv | **dry** | *adj.* sèk |
| | *v.* rèvé, rèv | **duck** | *n.* kanar |
| **dress** | *n.* ròb | **during** | *conj.* pendan |
| **dresser** | *n.* twalèt | **dust** | *n.* (la)poud |
| **drink** | *v.* bwa | | *n.* (la)pousyær |
| | *n.* bwason | **dwell** | *v.* rèsté, rès |
| **drop** | *n.* gout | | *v.* viv |

# E – e

| | | | |
|---|---|---|---|
| **each** | *adj.* shak | **end** | *n.* fin |
| **each other** | *n.* ènn-a-lòt | **end (of object)** | *n.* bout |
| **ear** | *n.* zòrèy | **end up** | *v.* sòrti, sòr |
| **ear of corn** | *nphr.* népi-mayi | **engaged** | *v, adj.* fyansé |
| **earache** | *n.* mal-zòrèy | **English language** | *n.* mérikin; nanglé |
| **early** | *adj.* bonnœr | **enjoy** | *v.* èndjòy |
| **earn** | *v.* ganñé, ganñ | **enough** | *adv.* asé |
| **earth** | *n.* (la)tær | **enter** | *v.* rentré, rent |
| **east** | *n, adj.* lès | **escape** | *v.* shapé, shap |
| **Easter** | *n.* Pak | **especially** | *adv.* surtou |
| **eastern** | *n, adj.* lès | **essentially** | *adv.* jolimen |
| **Eastern red cedar** | *n.* sipré | **even** | *adj.* minm |
| **easy** | *adj.* izé | **evening** | *n.* swaré |
| **eat** | *v.* manjé, manj | **eveningtime** | *n.* swaré |
| **eat (of animals)** | *v.* safré, saf | **ever** | *adv.* jamé |
| **eat breakfast** | *n, v.* déjœné, déjœn | **every** | *adj.* shak |
| **eat like an animal (of humans)** | *v.* safré, saf | **every day** | *adv.* touléjour |
| **eat lunch** | *n, v.* diné, dinn | **everybody** | *nphr.* toukèkènn |
| **economize** | *v.* ménajé, ménaj | **everyone** | *nphr.* toukèkènn |
| **egg** | *n.* (dé)zèf | | *nphr.* toumoun |
| **eggplant** | *n.* brenm | **everything** | *n.* toukishòj |
| **egret** | *n.* zégré | **evil** | *n.* mal |
| **eight** | *n.* wit | **example** | *n.* ègzamp |
| **eighteen** | *n.* diz-wit | **excellent** | *adj.* vayan |
| **eighty** | *n.* katré-vin | **excuse** | *v.* èskizé, èskiz |
| **either** | *adv.* non pli | **expensive** | *adj.* shær |
| **eleven** | *n.* onz | **explode** | *v.* èksplozé |
| **embarrass** | *v, adj.* embarasé | **extremely** | *adv.* foutimen |
| **empty** | *adj.* vid | **eye** | *n.* zyé |

# F – f

| | |
|---|---|
| **face** | *n.* (la)figur |
| **fall** | *n.* lotòn |
| | *v.* tombé, tomb |
| **false** | *adj.* fo |
| **family** | *n.* famiy |
| **far** | *adv, prep.* lwin |
| **farm** | *vphr.* fé rékòlt |
| **farmer** | *n.* (l)abitan |
| **fast** | *adj, adv.* vit |
| **fat** | *adj.* gro |
| **father** | *n.* pær |
| **father-in-law** | *n.* bo-pær |
| **fault** | *n.* (la)fot |
| **fear** | *n, v.* pœr |
| **February** | *n.* fèvriyé |
| **feel (reflexive)** | *v.* senti, sen |
| **female lover** | *n.* bèl |
| **field** | *n.* klo |
| **fifteen** | *n.* kinz |
| **fifty** | *n.* sinkant |
| **fifty-one** | *n.* sinkant-é-ènn |
| **fight** | *v.* bat |
| **filé** | *n.* filé |
| **fine** | *adj.* kòrèk |
| **finger** | *n.* dwa |
| **finish** | *v.* fini |
| **fire** | *n.* difé |
| **first** | *adj.* prèmyé |
| **fish** | *v.* péshé, pèsh |
| | *n.* pwason |
| **fisher** | *n.* péshœr |
| **fix** | *v.* ranjé, ranj |
| **flood** | *nphr.* dolo ho |
| **floor** | *n.* planshé |
| **floor (of a building)** | *n.* zétaj |
| **flower** | *n.* flœr |
| **flu** | *n.* (la)rimm |
| **fly** | *n.* (dé)moush |
| | *v.* volé, vòl |
| **follow** | *v.* swiv |
| **food** | *n.* manjé |
| **foolish** | *adj.* sòt |
| **foot** | *n.* pyé |
| **for** | *prep.* pou |
| **for example** | *exp.* par ègzamp |
| **for sure** | *advphr.* pou sûr |
| **forest** | *n.* foré |
| **forever** | *adv.* toultem |
| **forget** | *v.* bliyé, bliy |
| **forgive** | *v.* pardonné, pardonn |
| **fork (for eating)** | *n.* fourshèt |
| **forty** | *n.* karant |
| **four** | *n.* kat |
| **fourteen** | *n.* katòrz |
| **fourty-one** | *n.* karant-é-ènn |
| **Fr. 'donc'** | *interj.* alòr |
| **freeze** | *v.* jélé, jèl |
| **French** | *n.* Françé; françé |
| **fresh** | *adj.* frèsh |
| **fricassee** | *n, v.* frikasé, frikas |
| **Friday** | *n.* vendrédi |
| **friend** | *n.* (z)ami |
| | *n.* padna |
| **from** | *prep.* a |
| | *prep.* d(e) |
| **frost** | *n.* (la)glas |
| **fruit** | *n.* frwi |
| **fry** | *v.* fri |
| **frying pan** | *n.* (la)pwal |
| **full** | *adj, n.* plin |
| **fun** | *n.* fonn |
| **funny** | *adj.* dròl |
| **future marker** | *aux.* a |
| | *aux.* sa |
| | *aux.* va |

# G – g

| | |
|---|---|
| **gallivant** | *v.* rodayé, roday |
| **game** | *n.* gém |
| **gar (fish)** | *n.* pwason-armé |
| **garage** | *n.* garaj |
| **garden** | *n.* jardin |
| **garlic** | *n.* lay |
| **gasoline** | *n.* gazolinn |
| **gather** | *v.* ramasé, ramas |
| **gentleman** | *n.* misyé |
| **German** | *n, adj.* alman |
| **get** | *v.* trapé, trap |
| **get away** | *v.* shapé, shap |
| **get cold** | *v.* frédi |
| **get dirty** | *v.* barbouyé, barbouy<br>*v.* sali |
| **get drunk** | *v.* chaké, chak |
| **get fat** | *v.* grosi |
| **get off** | *v.* désenn |
| **get rid of** | *v.* jété, jèt |
| **get up** | *v.* lévé, lèv |
| **gift** | *n.* kado |
| **girl** | *n.* fiy |
| **girlfriend** | *n.* bèl<br>*n.* kalinn |
| **give** | *v.* donn |
| **give as a gift** | *vphr.* fé kado |
| **glass** | *n.* vær |
| **glass (for drinking)** | *n.* vær |
| **glasses** | *n.* linèt |
| **go** | *v.* alé<br>*v.* kouri |
| **go down** | *v.* désenn |
| **go grocery shopping** | *vphr.* fé grosri |
| **go out** | *v.* sòrti, sòr |
| **go to bed** | *v.* koushé, koush |
| **God** | *n.* Bondjè |
| **goddaughter** | *n.* fiyèl |
| **godfather** | *n.* parin |
| **godmother** | *n.* marènn |
| **godson** | *n.* fiyo |
| **gone** | *v, adj.* gonn |
| **good** | *adj.* bon<br>*adj, adv.* byin |
| **good evening** | *interj.* bonswa |
| **Good Friday** | *nphr.* Vendrédi Sin |
| **good night** | *interj.* bonswa |
| **goodbye** | *interj.* orévwar |
| **good-for-nothing** | *adj.* bonn-aryin |
| **goose** | *n.* (dé)zwa |
| **gossip** | *n.* kòmærs |
| **grandchild** | *n.* ti-zenfan, ti-piti |
| **granddaughter** | *n.* ti-fiy |
| **grandfather/grandpa** | *n.* gran-pær/gran-popa |
| **grandmother/grandma** | *n.* gran-mær/gran-moman |
| **grandparents** | *n.* gran-paren |
| **grandson** | *n.* ti-garçon |
| **grass** | *n.* zærb |
| **great** | *adj.* vayan |
| **great-grandchild** | *n.* gran-ti-zenfan |
| **green** | *adj.* vær |
| **green peas** | *n.* (dé)pwa |
| **grill** | *n.* gril<br>*v.* griyé, griy<br>*v.* roti |
| **grits** | *n.* digri |
| **grocery store** | *n.* (la)grosri |
| **ground** | *n.* (la)tær |
| **grow** | *v.* èlvé, (è)lèv<br>*v.* grandi<br>*v.* grosi<br>*v.* pousé, pous |
| **grow up** | *v.* grandi<br>*v.* grosi |
| **grow-up** | *n.* gran-moun |
| **guitar** | *n.* gita |
| **Gulf of Mexico** | *n.* Gòlf |
| **gumbo** | *n.* gombo |
| **gunpowder** | *n.* (la)poud |
| **guy** | *n.* boug |

# H - h

| | |
|---|---|
| **habitate** | *v.* rèsté, rès |
| **haha** | *onom.* kiki |
| **hair** | *n.* shévé |
| **half (used in telling time)** | |
| | *n.* demi |
| **half of** | *n.* (la)mòché |
| **half-brother** | *n.* mòché-fræ̀r |
| **half-sister** | *n.* mòché-sœr |
| **hand** | *n.* (la)min |
| **hang** | *v.* pònn |
| **happen** | *v.* arivé, ariv |
| **happy** | *adj.* konten |
| **Happy birthday!** | *phr.* Bonn fèt! |
| **hard** | *adj.* dur |
| **harden** | *v.* dursi |
| **harvest** | *n.* rékòlt |
| **hat** | *n.* shapo |
| **haul** | *v.* mènné, mènn |
| **have** | *v.* gin |
| **have nerve** | *vphr.* gin toupé |
| **have to** | *v.* dwa |
| | *vphr.* gin pou |
| **hay** | *n.* difwin |
| **he** | *pro.* li |
| **head** | *n.* (la)tèt |
| **headache** | *nphr.* mal-latèt/mal-de-tèt |
| **headscarf** | *n.* tiyon |
| **heal** | *v.* géri |
| **healthy** | *adj.* gayar |
| **hear** | *v.* tendé, tenn |
| **heart** | *n.* kœr |
| **heartburn** | *nphr.* brilmen-lèstoma |
| | *n.* mal-o-kœr |
| **heaven** | *n.* paradi |
| | *n.* syèl |
| **heavy** | *adj.* dri |
| | *adj.* lour |
| **hello** | *interj.* bonjou |
| **help** | *v.* édé, èd |
| **hen** | *n.* poul |
| **henhouse** | *n.* poulayé |
| **her** | *det.* sô |
| **her (object and subject pronoun)** | |
| | *pro.* èl |
| **herbal tea** | *n.* (la)tizann |
| **here** | *prep.* isit |
| | *prep, conj.* la |
| **heritage** | *n.* léritaj |
| **hey!** | *interj.* hé! |
| **hidden** | *v, adj.* kashé |
| **hide** | *v, adj.* kashé |
| **hip** | *n.* (la)hansh |
| **his** | *det.* sô |
| **hit** | *v.* koñé, koñ |
| **hoe** | *v.* pyoshé, pyòsh |
| **hold** | *v.* chombo |
| **holiday** | *n.* (la)fèt |
| **Holy Saturday** | *nphr.* Sammdi Sin |
| **honey** | *n.* dimyèl |
| **honeybee** | *n.* moush-a-myèl |
| **hope** | *v.* swaté, swat |
| **horn** | *n.* kòrn |
| **horse** | *n.* shval |
| **horseshoe** | *n.* fær-a-shwal |
| **hospital** | *n.* lopital |
| **hot** | *adj.* sho |
| **hour** | *n.* lœr |
| | *n.* zœr |
| **house** | *n.* (la)mézon |
| **how** | *conj.* komen |
| **how many** | *adv.* kombyin |
| **hug** | *v.* embrasé, embras |
| **humid** | *adj.* imid |
| **hungry** | *adj.* fim |
| **hunt** | *v.* shasé, shas |
| **hunting** | *n.* lashans |
| | *n.* lashas |
| **hurricane** | *n.* lòragan |
| **hurt** | *vphr.* fé mal |
| **husband** | *n.* mari |
| **husk** | *n.* (la)pay |

## I – i

| | |
|---|---|
| **I (subject)** | *pro.* mo |
| **ice** | *n.* (la)glas |
| **ice cream** | *n.* (la)glas |
| **idea** | *n.* nidé |
| **if** | *conj.* si |
| **Illinois** | *n.* Ozilinwa |
| **important** | *adj.* impòrtan |
| **impossible** | *adj.* impòsib |
| **in** | *prep.* dan |
| | *prep.* en |
| **in back** | *prep.* ennaryær |
| **in front of** | *prep.* dévan |
| | *prep.* ennavan |
| **Indian (Native American)** | *n, adj.* Zindyin; zindyin |
| **injure** | *v.* blésé, blès |
| **insect** | *nphr.* ti-bétay |
| **inside** | *prep.* endan |
| **intelligence** | *n.* lèspri |
| **interested** | *adj.* intérèsé |
| **interesting** | *adj.* intérèsé |
| **it** | *pro.* ça |
| | *pro.* li |
| **it was** | *vphr.* çé té |
| **Italian** | *n, adj.* italyin |
| **its** | *det.* sô |

## J – j

| | |
|---|---|
| **jacket** | *n.* jakèt |
| **jambalaya** | *n.* jambalaya |
| **January** | *n.* janvyé |
| **jazz** | *n, adj.* djaz |
| **Jewish** | *n, adj.* jwif |
| **job** | *n.* djòb |
| **joke** | *vphr.* fé fars |
| **joy** | *n.* (la)jwa |
| **jug** | *n.* djòg |
| **juice** | *n.* diji |
| **July** | *n.* jilyèt |
| **jumble** | *n.* galimacha |
| **June** | *n.* jwin |
| **just** | *adv.* jish |
| **justice** | *n.* (la)jistis |

## K – k

| | |
|---|---|
| **key** | *n.* (la)klé |
| **kill** | *v.* choué, chou |
| **kind** | *n.* kalité |
| **kind of** | *n, adv.* mòyær |
| **kindling** | *n.* branshaj |
| **kiss** | *v.* embrasé, embras |
| **kitchen** | *n.* (la)kizinn |
| **knee** | *n.* jnou |
| **knife** | *n.* kouto |
| **know** | *v.* koné |

# L - l

| | |
|---|---|
| **lady** | *n.* madamm |
| **lagniappe** | *n.* lañap |
| **lamp** | *n.* (la)lamp |
| **last** | *adj.* dærñær |
| **last (for a while)** | *v.* diré, dir |
| **late** | *adj.* tar |
| **lazy** | *n, adj.* kalin |
| | *adj.* parésé |
| **leaf** | *n.* féy |
| **learn** | *v.* aprenn |
| **leave** | *v, adj.* gonn |
| | *v.* kité, kit |
| | *v.* lésé, lès |
| | *v.* parti, par |
| **left** | *adv.* agosh |
| **left (as opposed to right)** | *adj.* gosh |
| **leg** | *n.* jamb |
| **leg or foot (of animal)** | *n.* (la)pat |
| **lemon** | *n.* limon |
| **Lent** | *n.* Karèm |
| **less** | *adv, n.* mwins |
| **lesson** | *n.* léçon |
| **let** | *v.* kité, kit |
| | *v.* lésé, lès |
| **let's** | *aux.* alon |
| **level** | *n.* nivo |
| **lie** | *v.* menti, men |
| **lie down** | *v.* koushé, koush |
| **life** | *n.* (la)vi |
| **light** | *adj.* léjé |
| | *n.* (la)limyær |
| **light (said of skin)** | *adj, adv.* klær |
| **lightning** | *n.* zéklær |
| **like** | *adj.* konm |
| | *v.* linmé, linm |
| **lip** | *n.* babìnn |
| **list** | *n.* lis |
| **listen** | *v.* kouté, kout |
| **little** | *adj.* piti |
| | *n.* ti |
| **little piece** | *n.* mòrso |
| **live** | *v.* rèsté, rès |
| | *v.* viv |
| **livestock** | *n.* bétay |
| **living** | *adj.* vivan |
| **living room** | *n.* salon |
| **lizard** | *n.* lézar |
| **lock** | *v.* aklé |
| | *v.* baré, bar |
| **lonesome** | *adj.* ennwiyé |
| **long time** | *adv.* lontem |
| **long time ago** | *advphr.* lontem pasé |
| **look at** | *v.* gardé, gar |
| | *v.* gété, gèt |
| **look for** | *v.* sharshé, sharsh |
| **look like** | *v.* senm |
| **lose** | *v.* pærd |
| **lost** | *adj.* pærdi |
| **lottery** | *n.* (la)lotri |
| **loud** | *adj.* fòr |
| **Louisiana** | *n.* (La)Lwizyann |
| **love** | *n.* (l)amour |
| | *v.* linmé, linm |
| **lover (female)** | *n.* kalinn |
| **lover (male)** | *n.* (l)amourè |
| | *n, adj.* kalin |
| **luck** | *n.* (la)shans |
| **lucky** | *phr.* gin lashans |
| **lunch** | *n, v.* dinné, dinn |
| | *n.* lonch |

# M – m

| | |
|---|---|
| **ma'am** | *n.* madamm |
| **machine** | *n.* mashinn |
| **mad** | *adj.* shoké |
| **make** | *v.* fé |
| **make a mess** | *vphr.* fé kòmærs |
| **make eyes (at)** | *vphr.* fé zyé dou (apré) |
| **make up one's mind** | *vphr.* fé sô nidé |
| **male genitalia** | *n.* klouk |
| **man** | *n.* boug |
| | *n.* nonm |
| **manage** | *v.* galopé, galòp |
| **manure** | *n.* fimyé |
| **many** | *adj, adv.* bokou |
| | *adj.* plizyær |
| **March** | *n.* mars |
| **Mardi Gras** | *n.* Karnaval |
| **marriage** | *n.* maryaj |
| **married name** | *n.* nom-d-maryaj |
| **marry** | *v.* mariyé, mari |
| **mass** | *n.* (la)mès |
| **May** | *n.* mé |
| **maybe** | *adv.* petèt |
| **me (object)** | *pro.* mò |
| **mean** | *v.* minn |
| | *adj.* vilin |
| **meat** | *n.* (la)vyann |
| **medicine** | *n.* médsinn |
| | *n.* rémèd |
| **meet** | *v.* jwènn |
| **meet (someone for the first time)** | *vphr.* fé lakònésans (avèk) |
| **melon** | *n.* (dé)mlon |
| **mess** | *n.* galimacha |
| **mile** | *n.* mil |
| **milk** | *n.* dilé |
| **mind** | *n.* nidé |
| **mint** | *n.* dibonm |
| **mischievious** | *adj.* kanay |
| **misery** | *n.* (la)mizær |
| **miss** | *v.* manké, mank |
| **mix** | *n.* méli-mélanj |
| | *v.* mélé, mèl |
| **mom** | *n.* moman |
| **Monday** | *n.* lindi |
| **money** | *n.* larjen |
| **moon** | *n.* (la)linn |
| **moral** | *n.* léçon |
| **more** | *adv, n.* pli(s) |
| **more...than** | *adjphr.* pli...ke |
| **mosquito** | *n.* maringwin |
| **mother** | *n.* mær |
| **mother-in-law** | *n.* bèl-mær |
| **motor** | *n.* mashinn |
| **mountain** | *n.* montañ |
| **mouth** | *n.* (la)boush |
| **mouth (informal)** | *n.* (la)djœl |
| **move** | *v.* grouyé, grouy |
| **move house** | *v.* déménajé, déménaj |
| **movie** | *n.* pòrtré |
| **Mr.** | *n.* misyé |
| **Mrs.** | *n.* madamm |
| **mud** | *n.* (la)bou |
| **mule** | *n.* milé |
| **music** | *n.* (la)mizik |
| **musical instrument** | *n.* linstrumen |
| **musician** | *n.* mizisyin |
| **must** | *v.* dwa |
| **mustache** | *n.* moustash |
| **mustard** | *n.* (la)moutard |
| **my** | *det.* mô |

# N – n

| | |
|---|---|
| **nail** | *n.* klou |
| | *v.* klouyé, klou |
| **name** | *n.* nom |
| **nap** | *n, v.* singgo |
| **nasty** | *adj.* vilin |
| **nation** | *n.* péyi |
| **Native American** | adj., n. Zindyin; zindyin |
| **natural** | *adj.* natirèl |
| **near** | *prep.* koté |
| | *prep.* ora |
| | *prep.* pré |
| | *adj, adv.* pròsh |
| **nearby** | *prep.* opré |
| **nearly** | *adj, adv.* pròsh |
| **neck** | *n.* kou |
| **need** | *v.* bezwin |
| **need to (do something)** | *phr.* ifo |
| **negative marker** | *conj.* pa |
| **neighbor (female)** | *n.* vwazinn |
| **neighbor (male or female)** | *n.* vwazin |
| **neighborhood** | *n.* vwazinaj |
| **nephew** | *n.* névé |
| **nest** | *n.* nik |
| **never** | *adv.* jamé |
| **new** | *adj.* nouvo |
| **New Orleans** | *n.* Lavil |
| | *n.* Nouvèl-Òrléan |
| | n. Envil |
| **next** | *adj.* proshin |
| **nice** | *adj.* vayan |
| **nickname** | *n.* ti-nom |
| **niece** | *n.* nyès |
| **night** | *n.* (la)nwit |
| **nightclub** | *n.* klœb |
| **nightmare** | *n.* koushmar |
| **nine** | *n.* nèf, nœf |
| **nineteen** | *n.* diz-nèf |
| **ninety** | *n.* katré-vin-dis |
| **no** | *interj.* non |
| **no one** | *n.* (pa) pærsonn |
| **noise** | *n.* trin |
| **noon** | *adv.* midi |
| **north** | *n, adj.* nòr |
| **nosy** | *adj.* kiriyé |
| **not** | *conj.* pa |
| **not at all** | *adv.* pa ditou |
| **not care** | *vphr.* fou pa mal |
| **not give a flyin' fiddlestick** | *vphr.* fou pa mal |
| **not much** | *adv.* pa gran-shòj |
| **not yet** | *adv.* pa enkòr |
| **nothing** | *n.* ariyin |
| **November** | *n.* novemb |
| **now** | *adv.* astœr |
| **now and then** | *adv.* tem-zen-tem |
| **nowhere** | *adv.* pa nil-plas |
| **number** | *n.* liméro/niméro |
| **nurse** | *v.* swonñé, swonñ |
| **nut** | *n.* nwa |

# O – o

| | |
|---|---|
| **o'clock** | *n.* lœr |
| | *n.* zœr |
| **occasionally** | *adv.* tem-zen-tem |
| **ocean** | *n.* (la)mær |
| **October** | *n.* oktòb |
| **of** | *prep.* a |
| | *prep.* d(e) |
| **office** | *n.* lofis |
| **often** | *adv.* souven |
| **oil** | *n.* lwil |

| | |
|---|---|
| **oilfield** | *n.* klo lwil |
| **okra** | *n.* févi |
| **old** | *adj.* vyé |
| **on** | *prep.* en |
| | *prep.* enho |
| | *adv, adj.* enlær |
| | *prep.* sur |
| **on top** | *prep.* dési |
| **one** | *n.* in |
| **onion** | *n.* zònyon |
| **open** | *v.* ouvri, ouvær |
| **or** | *conj.* ou |
| **orange (color)** | *n, adj.* zoranj |
| **orange (fruit)** | *n, adj.* zoranj |
| **other** | *adj.* dòt |
| | *adj.* lòt |
| **others** | *n.* (dé)zòt |
| **our** | *det.* nô |
| **out** | *adv, prep.* déyòr |
| **out of sorts** | *adj.* kagou |
| **outdoors** | *adv, prep.* déyòr |
| **outside** | *adv, prep.* déyòr |
| | *prep.* endéyòr |
| **outside of** | *prep.* endéyòr |
| **oven** | *n.* fou |
| **over** | *prep.* dési |
| **over there** | *prep.* laba |
| **owl** | *n.* ibou |
| **oyster** | *n.* (dé)zwit |

# P – p

| | |
|---|---|
| **Palm Sunday** | *nphr.* Dimansh Ramo |
| **pan** | *n.* shodyær |
| **pantry** | *n.* gar-manjé |
| | *n.* (la)kav |
| **pants** | *n.* kilot |
| | *n.* pantalon |
| **parent** | *n.* paren |
| **party** | *n.* (la)fèt |
| **pass** | *v.* pasé, pas |
| **pass away** | *v.* pasé, pas |
| **past marker** | *aux.* té |
| **path** | *n.* shmin |
| **paw** | *n.* (la)pat |
| **pay** | *v.* péyé, péy |
| **peace** | *n.* lapé |
| **peaceful** | *adj.* trankil |
| **pear** | *n.* (dé)pwar |
| **pecan** | *n.* pakònn |
| **pee** | *v, n.* pipi |
| **pelican** | *n.* pélikan |
| **pepper (vegetable)** | *n.* pimen |
| **persimmon** | *n.* plakminn |
| **person** | *n.* moun |
| **pho (Vietnamese soup)** | *n.* fò |
| **phone** | *n.* fonn |
| **photo** | *n.* pòrtré |
| **pick up** | *v.* ramasé, ramas |
| **picture** | *n.* pòrtré |
| **pie** | *n.* pay |
| **pig** | *n.* koshon |
| **pink** | *adj.* roz |
| **pitchfork** | *n.* foursh |
| **place** | *n.* plas |
| **plain** | *n.* plènn |
| **plant** | *n.* plant |
| | *v.* planté, plant |
| **plate** | *n.* pla |
| **play** | *v.* joué, jou |
| **please** | *interj.* sitoplé, sivouplé |
| | *interj.* tanpri |
| **pleasure** | *n.* plézir |
| **plural marker** | *det.* -yé |
| **police** | *n.* polis |
| **poop** | *v, n.* kaka |
| **poor** | *adj.* maléré |
| **popcorn** | *n.* taktak |

| | |
|---|---|
| **porch** | *n.* (la)galri |
| **possum** | *n.* ra-d-bwa |
| **pot** | *n.* shodyær |
| **potato** | *n.* patat |
| **pound (unit of measurement)** | |
| | *n.* liv |
| **powder** | *n.* (la)poud |
| **prairie** | *n.* pléri |
| **pray** | *vphr.* fé (sô) lapriyè |
| | *v.* priyé, priy |
| **prefer** | *vphr.* vo myé |
| **pregnant** | *adj.* enfamiy |
| **prepare** | *v.* ranjé, ranj |
| **pretty** | *adj.* joli |

| | |
|---|---|
| **pretty much** | *adv.* jolimen |
| **prevent** | *v.* péshé, pèsh |
| **prison** | *n.* prizon |
| **problem** | *n.* traka |
| **progress** | *v.* avansé, avans |
| **progressive marker** | *aux.* ap(é) |
| **promise** | *v.* promèt |
| | *n.* særmen |
| **protect** | *v.* protéjé, protèj |
| **proud** | *adj.* fyær |
| **pure** | *adj.* pur |
| **push** | *v.* pousé, pous |
| **put** | *v.* mèt |
| **put on** | *v.* mèt |

## Q – q

| | |
|---|---|
| **question** | *n.* kèstyon |
| **quickly** | *adj, adv.* vit |

| | |
|---|---|
| **quiet** | *v.* pé |
| | *adj.* trankil |

## R – r

| | |
|---|---|
| **raccoon** | *n.* shawi |
| **race** | *n.* (la)ras |
| **rain** | *v.* mouyé, mouy |
| | *n.* (la)pli |
| **raise** | *v.* èlvé, (è)lèv |
| | *v.* lévé, lèv |
| **rare** | *adj.* rar |
| **rat** | *n.* ra |
| **read** | *v.* lir |
| **ready** | *adj.* paré |
| **refrigerator** | *n.* glasyær |
| **relative** | *n.* paren |
| **relax (sometimes reflexive)** | |
| | *v.* (ré)pozé, (ré)poz |
| **relief** | *n.* (la)frèsh |
| **remain** | *v.* rèsté, rès |
| **remedy** | *n.* rémèd |
| **remember** | *v.* raplé, rapèl |

| | |
|---|---|
| **remove** | *v.* oté, ot |
| **rent** | *v.* loué, lou |
| **repair** | *v.* ranjé, ranj |
| **respect** | *n.* rèspé |
| | *v.* rèspèkté, rèspèk |
| **respond** | *v.* réponn |
| **response** | *n.* répons |
| **rest** | *v.* (ré)pozé, (ré)poz |
| **return** | *v.* rentré, rent |
| **rice** | *n.* diri |
| **ride** | *v.* monté, mont |
| **right** | *adj, n.* drwa |
| | *vphr/adjphr.* gin rézon |
| **right (direction)** | *adv.* adrwa |
| **right here** | *prep.* drèt-la |
| **right then** | *prep.* drèt-la |
| **ripe** | *adj.* mir |
| **river** | *n.* (la)rivyær |

| | |
|---|---|
| **road** | *n.* shmin |
| **roam** | *v.* rodayé, roday |
| **roast** | *v.* griyé, griy |
| | *v.* roti |
| **roof** | *n.* twa |
| **room** | *n.* (la)sal |
| | *n.* shanm |
| **rooster** | *n.* korish |
| **run** | *v.* galopé, galòp |
| **run one's mouth** | *vphr.* galopé laboush |
| **rusted** | *adj.* rouyé |
| **rusty** | *adj.* rouyé |

# S – s

| | |
|---|---|
| **sad** | *adj.* maléré |
| | *adj.* shagrin |
| | *adj.* tris |
| **salad** | *n.* (la)salad |
| **salt** | *v, adj.* salé |
| **salted** | *v, adj.* salé |
| **same** | *adj.* minm |
| | *adj.* paréy |
| **sassafras** | *n.* sasafra |
| **Saturday** | *n.* sanmdi |
| **sauce** | *n.* (la)sòs |
| **sausage** | *n.* sosis |
| **save** | *v.* sové, sov |
| **say** | *v.* di |
| **say (one's) prayers** | *vphr.* fé (sô) lapriyè |
| **school** | *n.* lékòl |
| **scratch** | *v.* graté, grat |
| **season** | *n.* (la)sézon |
| | *v, adj.* sézonné, sézonn |
| **seasoned** | *v, adj.* sézonné, sézonn |
| **second** | *adj.* dèzyèm |
| **see** | *v.* war |
| **seed** | *n.* grènn |
| **seek** | *v.* sharshé, sharsh |
| **seem** | *vphr.* gin lè |
| | *v.* senm |
| **seem like** | *v.* gardé, gar |
| **sell** | *v.* venn |
| **send** | *v.* voyé, vòy |
| **September** | *n.* sèptemb |
| **seven** | *n.* sèt |
| **seventeen** | *n.* dis-sèt |
| **seventy** | *n.* swasant-dis |
| **seventy-one** | *n.* swasant-onz |
| **shade** | *n.* (la)frèsh |
| | *n.* (l)ombraj |
| **shake** | *v.* grouyé, grouy |
| **shame** | *n.* domaj |
| | *n.* hont |
| **share** | *v.* partajé, partaj |
| **shatter** | *v.* brizé, briz |
| **she** | *pro.* èl |
| | *pro.* li |
| **sheep** | *n.* mouton |
| **shell** | *v.* kasé, kas |
| | *n.* kokiy |
| **shelter** | *n.* (l)abri |
| **shine** | *v.* briyé, briy |
| **ship** | *n.* batimen |
| **shirt** | *n.* shimij |
| **shoes** | *n.* soulyé |
| **short** | *adj.* kout |
| **shorts** | *nphr.* kilot kout |
| **shoulder** | *n.* zépol |
| **shout** | *v.* hélé, hèl |
| **show** | *v.* montré, mont |
| **shrimp** | *n.* shevrèt |
| **shuck** | *v.* kasé, kas |
| **shut** | *v.* færmé, færm |
| **shut up** | *v.* pé |
| **sick** | *adj.* malad |
| **sign** | *n.* nòtis |
| | *n.* siñ |
| **similar** | *adj.* paréy |

| | |
|---|---|
| **sin** | *v.* péshé, pèsh |
| **since** | *prep.* dépi |
| **sing** | *v.* shanté, shant |
| **sinner** | *n.* péshœr |
| **sir** | *n.* misyé |
| **sister** | *n.* sœr |
| **sister-in-law** | *n.* bèl-sœr |
| **sit** | *v.* asit |
| **six** | *n.* sis |
| **sixteen** | *n.* sèz |
| **sixty** | *n.* swasant |
| **sixty-one** | *n.* swasant-é-ènn |
| **skin** | *n.* (la)po |
| **sky** | *n.* syèl |
| **sleep** | *v.* dòrmi, dòr |
| **slime** | *n.* (la)gli |
| **slow** | *adj, adv.* dousmen |
| **slowly** | *adj, adv.* dousmen |
| **sly** | *adj.* kanay |
| | *adj.* malin |
| **small** | *adj.* piti |
| | *n.* ti |
| **smart** | *adj.* smat |
| **smell** | *v.* senti, sen |
| **smoke** | *n.* (la)boukònn |
| **smoke (meat)** | *v, adj.* boukònné |
| **smoke tobacco** | *v.* fimé, fimm |
| **smoked** | *v, adj.* boukònné |
| **smother** | *v.* étoufé, étouf |
| **snapping turtle** | *n.* kawènn |
| **sneeze** | *v.* étærné, étærn |
| **snow** | *v.* néjé, nèj |
| | *n.* (la)nèj |
| **so** | *interj.* alòr |
| | *conj.* ça-fé |
| | *conj.* si |
| | *adj, adv.* tan |
| **so (discourse particle)** | |
| | *interj.* so |
| **so (to emphasize an adjective)** | |
| | *adv.* si tèlmen |
| **so many** | *adv.* si tèlmen |
| | *adj, adv.* tan |
| **so much** | *adv.* si tèlmen |

| | |
|---|---|
| **sofa** | *n.* sofa |
| **some** | *adj.* dê |
| | *adj.* kèk |
| | *adjphr.* zen (dê) |
| **someone** | *pro.* kèkènn |
| **someone else** | *pro.* kèkènn dòt |
| **something** | *n.* kèk zafær |
| | *n.* kishòj |
| **sometimes** | *adv.* défwa |
| **somewhere** | *n.* kèk plas |
| **son** | *n.* garçon |
| **song** | *n.* shanson |
| **son-in-law** | *n.* bo-fis |
| **soon** | *adv.* talœr |
| **sore throat** | *nphr.* mal-lagòrj/mal-de-gòrj |
| **sorry** | *adj.* dézolé |
| | *adj.* shagrin |
| **sort** | *n.* kalité |
| **so-so** | *adjphr.* konm-çi-konm-ça |
| | *adj.* pokapok |
| **soul** | *n.* namm |
| **soup** | *n.* (la)soup |
| **south** | *n, adj.* sid |
| **southeast** | *n, adj.* sidès |
| **sow** | *v.* sinmé, sinm |
| **space** | *n.* plas |
| **Spanish** | *adj., n.* spañol |
| **speak** | *v.* parlé, parl |
| **spice** | *n.* épis |
| | *v, adj.* pimenté |
| **spiced** | *v, adj.* pimenté |
| **spicy** | *v, adj.* pimenté |
| **spider** | *n.* zaryin |
| **spin records** | *v.* spìnn |
| **spirit** | *n.* lèspri |
| **spit** | *v.* krashé, krash |
| **splash around** | *v.* patouyé, patouy |
| **spoon** | *n.* kiyær |
| **spring** | *n.* printem |
| **squirrel** | *n.* kiréy |
| **stagger** | *v.* baloté, balot |
| **staircase** | *n.* lèskalyé |
| **stairs** | *n.* lèskalyé |
| **standing** | *adj, adv.* débout |

| | |
|---|---|
| **star** | *n.* létwal |
| **start** | *v.* komensé, komens |
| **state** | *n.* léta |
| **stay** | *v.* rèsté, rès |
| **stay out late gallivanting** | *vphr.* fé lougarou |
| **steal** | *v.* volé, vòl |
| **stepfather** | *n.* bo-pær |
| **stepmother** | *n.* bèl-mær |
| **stew** | *v.* étoufé, étouf |
| | *n, v.* frikasé, frikas |
| | *n, v.* frikasé, frikas |
| **stick** | *n.* baton |
| **sticker** | *n.* pikan |
| **still** | *adv.* stìl |
| | *adj, adv.* toujou |
| **sting** | *v.* mòrd |
| **stomach** | *n.* lèstoma |
| | *n.* vent |
| **stomach ache** | *n.* mal-o-vent |
| **stop** | *v.* arété, arèt |
| **store** | *n.* boutik |
| | *n.* sto |
| **storm** | *n.* gro tem/mové tem |
| | *n.* lòragan |
| **story** | *n.* listwar |
| **stove** | *n.* stov |
| **straw** | *n.* (la)pay |
| **strike** | *v.* koñé, koñ |
| **string** | *n.* fil |
| **strong** | *adj.* fòr |
| **student** | *n.* étidyan |
| **study** | *v.* étidyé, étidi |
| **stupid** | *adj, n.* bèt |
| **such** | *adj.* tèl |
| **such and such** | *nphr.* tèl-é-tèl |
| **suck** | *v.* sisé, sis |
| **sugar** | *n.* disik |
| **sugarcane** | *n.* (dé)kann |
| **summer** | *n.* lété |
| **sun** | *n.* soléy |
| **Sunday** | *n.* dimansh |
| **sunfish** | *n.* patasa |
| **sunrise** | *n.* soléy-lévé |
| **sunset** | *n.* soléy-koushé |
| **super** | *adj.* supærb |
| **supper** | *n.* soupé |
| **suppose** | *v.* sipozé, sipòz |
| **supposed to** | *aux.* sipozé (pou) |
| **sure** | *adj.* sûr |
| **surname** | *n.* nom-d-famiy |
| **surprised** | *adj.* étòné |
| **swamp** | *n.* sipriyær |
| **swear** | *n.* særmen |
| | *vphr.* fé særmen |
| **sweat** | *v.* swé |
| **sweep** | *v.* balé, bal |
| **sweet** | *adj.* dou |
| **sweet potato** | *n.* patat |
| | *n.* patat dous |
| **swim** | *v.* bèñé, bèñ |
| | *v.* najé, naj |
| **syrup** | *n.* siro |

# T – t

| | |
|---|---|
| **table** | *n.* (la)tab |
| **tail** | *n.* (la)ké |
| **take** | *v.* prenn |
| **take off** | *v.* oté, ot |
| **tall** | *adj.* gran |
| **taste** | *v.* gouté, gou |
| **tea** | *n.* dité |
| **teach** | *v.* aprenn |
| | *v.* montré, mont |
| **teacher (female)** | *nphr.* métrès |
| **teacher (male)** | *nphr.* mèt-(d)-lékol/mèt |
| **tell** | *v.* di |

| | |
|---|---|
| **ten** | *n.* dis |
| **Texas** | *n.* Tèksas |
| **than** | *conj.* ke |
| **thanks** | *interj.* mærsi; mèsi |
| **that** | *pro.* ça |
| | *det.* -çala |
| | *conj.* ke |
| **that (in relative clauses)** | |
| | *conj.* ki |
| **the** | *det.* -la |
| | *det.* la, le, lê |
| **the bottom** | *prep.* ofon |
| **their** | *det.* yê |
| **then** | *interj.* alòr |
| | *prep, conj.* la |
| | *conj.* pi |
| **there** | *prep, conj.* la |
| | *prep.* laba |
| **there is/are** | *vphr.* ina |
| **there was/were** | *vphr.* inavé |
| **there will be** | *vphr.* nora |
| **these** | *det.* -çi(la)yé |
| **they** | *pro.* ça |
| **they (subject and object)** | |
| | *pro.* yé |
| **thick (with)** | *adj.* dri |
| **thin** | *adj.* léjé |
| **thing** | *n.* kishòj |
| | *n.* zafær |
| **think** | *v.* krò |
| | *v.* pensé, pens |
| **think about** | *v.* jonglé, jong (pou/enho/apré) |
| **thirsty** | *adj.* swaf |
| **thirteen** | *n.* trèz |
| **thirty** | *n.* trent |
| **thirty-one** | *n.* trent-é-ènn |
| **this** | *det.* -çila |
| **thorn** | *n.* pikan |
| **those** | *det.* -ça(la)yé |
| **though (discourse particle)** | |
| | *interj.* do |
| **thought** | *n.* nidé |
| **thousand** | *n.* mil |
| **three** | *n.* trò |
| **throw** | *v.* garoshé, garòsh |
| | *v.* jété, jèt |
| | *v.* voyé, vòy |
| **throw a party** | *vphr.* fé sosyété |
| **throw up** | *v.* rèshté, rèshèt |
| **thunder** | *n.* tònær |
| **Thursday** | *n.* jœdi |
| **ticket** | *n.* tikèt |
| **tiger** | *n.* tig |
| **tignon** | *n.* tiyon |
| **time** | *n.* fwa |
| | *n.* tem |
| **tired** | *adj.* las |
| **to** | *prep.* a |
| | *prep.* pou |
| **toad** | *n.* krapo |
| **tobacco** | *n.* taba |
| **today** | *n.* jòrdi |
| **toe** | *n.* zòrtèy |
| **together** | *adj.* ensenm |
| **toilet** | *n.* komod |
| **tomato** | *n.* tomat |
| **tomorrow** | *n.* démin |
| **tongue** | *n.* (la)lanng |
| **tonight** | *n.* aswa |
| **too** | *conj.* itou |
| | *conj.* osit |
| | *adj.* tro |
| **too many** | *nphr.* tro bokou |
| **too much** | *nphr.* tro bokou |
| **tool** | *n.* zouti |
| **tooth** | *n.* den |
| **toothache** | *n.* mal-o-den |
| **town** | *n.* vilaj |
| **trail** | *v.* trènné, trènn |
| **train** | *n.* trin |
| **trap** | *v.* trapé, trap |
| **travel** | *v.* vwayajé, vwayaj |
| **travel on the road** | *v.* rodayé, roday |
| **traveller** | *n.* rodayœr |
| **treasure** | *n.* trézòr |
| **tree** | *n.* narb |

| | | | |
|---|---|---|---|
| **trip** | *n.* vwayaj | **turn (an age)** | *vphr.* fé zan |
| **trouble** | *n.* (la)mizær | **turn out bad** | *vphr.* sòrti salé |
| | *n.* traka | **twelve** | *n.* douz |
| **truck** | *n.* tròk | **twenty** | *n.* vin |
| **true** | *adj.* vré | **twenty-one** | *n.* vint-é-ènn |
| **trust** | *v.* tròs | **twenty-two** | *n.* vin-dé |
| **try** | *v.* séyé, séy | **twigs** | *n.* branshaj |
| **Tuesday** | *n.* mardi | **two** | *n.* dé |
| **turn** | *v.* tòrné, tòrn | **type** | *n.* kalité |

# U – u

| | | | |
|---|---|---|---|
| **ugly** | *adj.* lèd | **until** | *prep.* jiska |
| | *adj.* vilin | **up** | *adv, adj.* enlær |
| **uncle** | *n.* nonk | **upset** | *v.* boulværsé, boulværs |
| **under** | *prep.* enba | **us (object)** | *pro.* nou, nouzòt |
| **understand** | *v.* komprenn | **USA** | *n.* Létazini |
| **underwear** | *n.* kalçon | **use** | *v.* izé, iz |
| **unfortunate** | *adj.* maléré | | *v.* særvi, sær |
| **unfortunately** | *adv.* malèrèzmen | **use sparingly** | *v.* ménajé, ménaj |
| **unique** | *adj.* inik | **used to** | *aux.* abichud |
| **unruly** | *adj, n.* dézòrd | **useful** | *adj.* itil |
| **untamed** | *adj.* faroush | | |

# V – v

| | | | |
|---|---|---|---|
| **vegetables** | *n.* jardinaj | **visit (person or place)** | |
| **very** | *adj, adv.* bokou | | *v.* vizité, vizit |
| | *adj, adv.* byin | **voice** | *n.* (la)vwa |
| **vicinity** | *n.* vwazinaj | **voilà** | *interj.* vwala |
| **video** | *n.* vidyo | **vomit** | *v.* rèshté, rèshèt |
| **vinegar** | *n.* vinég | | *v.* vomi |
| **violet (color)** | *n, adj.* vyolèt | **voyage** | *n.* vwayaj |
| **violet (flower)** | *n, adj.* vyolèt | **vulture** | *n.* karankro |

# W - w

| | |
|---|---|
| **wait (for)** | *v.* spéré, èspær (pou) |
| **walk** | *v.* marshé, marsh |
| **wall** | *n.* (la)miray |
| **want** | *v.* olé |
| | *v.* ve |
| **warn** | *v.* aværti |
| **was** | *aux.* té |
| **wash** | *v.* lavé, lav |
| **wasp** | *n.* djèp |
| **watch** | *v.* gardé, gar |
| | *v.* gèté, gèt |
| **water** | *n.* dolo |
| **way (of doing)** | *n, adv.* mòyær |
| **we (subject)** | *pro.* no, nouzòt |
| **weak** | *adj.* fèb |
| **wear** | *v.* pòrté, pòrt |
| **weather** | *n.* tem |
| **Wednesday** | *n.* mærkrédi |
| **week** | *n.* (la)smènn |
| **weekend** | *n.* fin-lasmèn |
| **weird** | *adj.* dròl |
| **well** | *adj, adv.* byin |
| **well (discourse particle)** | |
| | *interj.* wèl |
| **werewolf** | *n.* lougarou |
| **west** | *n, adj.* wès |
| **wet** | *v.* mouyé, mouy |
| **what** | *pro.* ça |
| | *conj.* kèl |
| | *conj.* ki |
| | *conj.* kwa |
| **what...?** | *conj.* ça...? |
| | *conj.* kèl...? |
| | *conj.* ki ça...? |
| | *conj.* ki çé...? |
| | *conj.* ki...? |
| **whatever** | *adj, n.* nimpòrt (ki) |
| **when** | *adv, conj.* ékan |
| | *adv, conj.* kan |
| **where** | *conj.* éyou |
| **which** | *conj.* kèl |
| **whichever** | *adj, n.* nimpòrt (ki) |
| **while** | *conj.* pendan |
| | *conj.* tandi |
| **whiskey** | *n.* wiski |
| **whistle** | *v.* siflé, sif |
| **white** | *adj.* blan |
| **whitewash** | *v.* blanshi |
| **who** | *conj.* ki |
| | *conjphr.* ki moun |
| **why** | *conj.* kòfær |
| **wide open** | *adjphr.* gran-ouvær |
| **wife** | *n.* fenm |
| | *n.* madamm |
| **wild** | *adj, n.* dézòrd |
| | *adj.* faroush |
| **will** | *aux.* va |
| **will be** | *aux.* sa |
| **willow tree** | *n.* sol |
| **wilt** | *v.* fònné, fònn |
| **win** | *v.* ganñé, ganñ |
| **wind** | *n.* diven |
| **window** | *n.* (la)finèt |
| **wine** | *n.* divin |
| **winter** | *n.* livær |
| **wire** | *n.* fil |
| **wish** | *v.* swaté, swat |
| **with** | *conj.* avèk |
| **without** | *conj.* san |
| **woman** | *n.* fenm |
| **womanizer** | *n.* siro |
| **wonderful** | *adj.* supærb |
| **wood** | *n.* dibwa |
| **woods** | *n.* dibwa |

| | |
|---|---|
| **word** | *n.* paròl |
| **work** | *n.* louvraj |
| | *n.* ouvraj |
| | *n.* travay |
| | *v.* travayé, travay |
| **worm** | *n.* (dé)vær |
| **worry** | *v.* trakasé, trakas |
| **worth** | *v.* vo |
| **would be** | *aux.* sé |
| **would be better** | *vphr.* vo myé |
| **wow!** | *interj.* yéyay! |
| **write** | *v.* ékri |

# Y – y

| | |
|---|---|
| **yard** | *n.* (la)kour |
| **year** | *n.* (l)ané |
| **year (for counting age)** | *n.* (z)an |
| **year (when counting or with a number)** | *n.* zan |
| **yell** | *v.* hèlé, hèl |
| **yellow** | *adj.* jonn |
| **yes** | *interj.* wi |
| **yesterday** | *adv.* yær |
| **yet** | *adj, adv.* enkòr |
| **yeyaille!** | *interj.* yéyay! |
| **you (object)** | *pro.* twa |
| **you (plural) (subject and object)** | *pro.* (vou)zòt |
| **you (subject)** | *pro.* to |
| **you're welcome** | *phr.* pa-d-kwa |
| **young** | *adj.* jœn |
| **your (polite)** | *det.* vô |
| **your (singular)** | *det.* tô |

# Z – z

| | |
|---|---|
| **zydeco** | *n, adj.* zariko |

# More Resources

## *Books & Websites*

# *POU APRENN PLIS.* TO LEARN MORE.

Here are some more books and websites which we find very useful. We have chosen resources which should be easy to access. Check your local library for a copy of the books, if they don't have them then you could ask them to order them for you. These are also available to purchase in bookstores and online.

### *LIV.* BOOKS.

Klingler, Thomas A. *If I Could Turn My Tongue like That: The Creole Language of Pointe Coupee Parish, Louisiana.* Baton Rouge: Louisiana State University Press, 2003.

Professor Thomas A. Klingler describes the variety of Creole spoken in Pointe Coupée in detail. This is a technical linguistic study including a bunch of very interesting information about the language's history and grammar.

Neumann, Ingrid. *Le Créole de Breaux Bridge, Louisiane: Étude Morphosyntaxique, Textes, Vocabulaire.* Hamburg: Helmut Buske Verlag, 1985.

This book was once out of print, but Professor Ingrid Neumann-Holzschuh re-released this book in 2018 by popular request! Professor Neumann-Holzschuh documented the Creole of Breaux Bridge in the 1980s, and wrote this detailed technical description in French.

Valdman, Albert, Thomas A. Klingler, Margaret M. Marshall, and Kevin J. Rottet. *Dictionary of Louisiana Creole.* Bloomington: Indiana University Press, 1998.

Built on at least a decade of field research, this is a large, comprehensive dictionary of Louisiana Creole. Sadly now out of print, but you can order a e-book copy here from Indiana University Center for Latin American and Caribbean Studies. More information is available here: www.indiana.edu/~creole/index.shtml

**PLAS LATWAL. WEBSITES.**

The *Kouri-Vini Louisiana Creole Language Fanpage* on Facebook is the home of the language online. Come meet new friends, practice what you've learned, and study with us! facebook.com/Kourivini

*Louisiana Historical and Cultural Vistas* is Dr. Christophe Landry's website for all things Louisiana – including a web store, a lively blog and tons of information on history, culture, Louisiana languages, and genealogy: mylhcv.com

Alcée Fortier's *Louisiana Folk Tales: In French Dialect and English Translation* are available online: archive.org/details/ajs8769.0001.001.umich.edu or search for 'Fortier Louisiana Folk Tales Archive.org'

There is a digitized version of the *Dictionary of Louisiana Creole*, converted to the orthography used in this book, available here: louisianacreoledictionary.com

The *Atlas of Pidgin and Creole Language Structures Online* has a technical description of Louisiana Creole written by Professor Thomas A. Klingler and Professor Ingrid Neumann-Holzschuh, which includes references to more books and academic papers if you want even more to read! apics-online.info/surveys/53

Printed in Poland
by Amazon Fulfillment
Poland Sp. z o.o., Wrocław

65875519R00100